Lit

'A friend is a gift you give yourself' – and never is that more true than of Lou and Esther, who are there for each other in joy and heartbreak, dieting and shopping, love and the laundry. But don't be deceived. Embedded in this wry, witty and revealingly frank correspondence is many a buried gem of wisdom on the basic, gritty issues of life that make us laugh and make us cry, and that we survive by sharing.

Michele Guinness, author and speaker

Really brilliant! We're allowed to eavesdrop on indiscreet conversations. All the tricky issues facing women in churches are likely to be included in these hilarious conversations! This should be on every leader's 'must read' list.

Joel Edwards, International Director, Micah Challenge

A down-to-earth, no-holds-barred ongoing email conversation between two devoted friends from very different backgrounds. One married with children, the other single, they support and encourage each other in a very real way through problems great and small, with humour and compassion.

Fiona Castle OBE, author, presenter and speaker

Refreshingly different. You get the chance to read the letters and texts between two friends and find yourself smiling as you recognize yourself! This book also has a way of making you feel good about yourself, and I love that.

Debra Green OBE, Founder & National Director ROC

A witty and engaging book charting some of the trials and tribulations of Christendom. A fun read.

Liz Babbs, author and humorist

Life Lines

Two Friends Sharing Laughter,
Challenges and Cupcakes

Deborah Duncan and Cathy Le Feuvre

Authentic

First published 2014 by Authentic Media Limited,
52 Presley Way, Crownhill, Milton Keynes, MK8 0ES.
authenticmedia.co.uk

British Library Cataloguing in Publication Data

A catalogue record for this book is available from the British Library.

ISBN 978-1-86024-930-3
e-book 978-1-78078-248-5

Cover design by David McNeill revocreative.co.uk
Printed and bound in Great Britain by Bell and Bain Ltd, Glasgow

To the many millions of women in this world, and in our churches, who just get on with life – whatever it throws at them – and also find time to laugh at themselves.

For our wonderful families, without whose support and encouragement this book would never have been possible.

ACKNOWLEDGEMENTS

Debbie: Thank you Malcolm, Matthew, Benjamin, Anna and Riodhna for your love, support and putting up with my mad days. You know I have always wanted to be a writer and you've helped me achieve that dream. Thanks also to Mum, Dad and the rest of the family – I'm so blessed to have you! Lorna and Paul, thank you for your encouragement.

Cathy: Thanks to my fabulous mum – a real positive Christian role model – and to my extended family, wherever you are in the world, for all your support and encouragement. Knowing people believe in you creates confidence and being part of such a loving family is vital to my sanity.

Thank you, too, to all our close friends who walk this journey with us – you know who you are. And a huge thanks to Amy Boucher Pye, our editor, for believing in Esther and Louise.

CONTENTS

Contents

AN INTRODUCTION FROM THE AUTHORS

This is an ordinary story of two friends who share their lives the way most of us do today – not just when they meet up for lunches, shopping and chats but also 'virtually' through email, text, phone and social media.

Cyberspace is packed with the stories of people's lives – some reflecting happy times like the birth of a child, a marriage or a professional achievement, and some tinged with pain as we share news of personal setbacks and sadness, unwanted illness and other traumas.

This is simply the story of two people who support each other in their everyday walking around lives, sharing the good times and the bad, the experiences that make their hearts soar, and the moments when they feel they are living on different planets to those around them. This story may be birthed in the realm of fiction but it vibrates in the real world we live in and we hope it will resonate with you. We wrote it to make you laugh and think.

So let us set the scene . . .

Louise and Esther go back a long way. They met at a student youth camp many moons ago and then reconnected when, coincidentally, Louise and Jack moved into Esther's town soon after they married. Louise is a woman juggling home, church and work life. She is 38, a mother of three wonderful and troublesome teenagers and is married to Jack who is an elder in their local church. She runs her own business making cupcakes from her kitchen but, like many creative entrepreneurs, dreams of bigger things. Her best friend, Esther, is 42, and as we join their story, her engagement to The One . . . well, the man who she thought was The One . . . has just come to an end. In her professional life as a successful self-employed PR consultant, Esther is accepted and respected for who she is but she is struggling with her identity in church. If you recognize yourself in Esther or Louise, or any of the friends, family members or acquaintances in their story then it's not intentional. Although we draw on real life, if we were a film we'd have a disclaimer . . . 'This is a work of fiction and any resemblance of characters to actual persons, living or dead, is purely coincidental.'

So please, sit back, dive in and enjoy!

1

SUBJECT: WHAT A DISASTER!

DATE: 5 FEBRUARY

Dear Louise

Quelle disastre!

I went to that Christian Valentine's evening thing last night . . . even though it's not yet the 14th! As I think I mentioned, it was the 'do' organized by all the churches in the area for all the sad singles. Much against my better judgement, because I should have known better, I was persuaded. Our Rev Tracey felt our church should be represented so she rounded up a little group. We agreed to meet and go together – safety in numbers.

Only three of us turned up! Rev T (who will be first to admit that she's not particularly looking for a fella at the moment since she's just turned 68 and is quite comfortable with her singlehood) and Leggy Lynda. You've met her. She could be wearing a bin liner and she'd still look fabulous. And then there was me! OK I was wearing my posh frock but I felt . . . well I'll just say it . . . alongside Lynda, I felt like I was wearing a tent, or, more accurately, a marquee!

So this was billed as a 'singles evening'. It was a nice hotel – The Ballroom, which is very swish but overstated. There was not much of a ballroom but we enjoyed a nice dinner matched by the nice price. Plus, truth be told, given the recent events in my life, I didn't go with any particular thought that Mr Right might scoop me up there and then. I really did feel that I was making up the numbers and I wasn't in a great mood.

But . . . well . . . the whole thing was simply HIDEOUS.

Half the people there weren't even single. There were couples, or would-be couples, everywhere. And most others appeared to be just on the prowl.

Everyone was GORGEOUS. Leggy Lyndas all over the shop! The St Michael's Mob was out in force and you know what they're like. Unless you're model material there's little point attending THAT church. I actually don't think I've ever seen an unattractive person come out of those doors – and that's just the team of pastors. From the start of the evening, I felt like slinking into a corner and putting my (rather expensive silk) shawl over my head so I could become invisible!

Firstly, I got stuck on a table with several of the most boring people in the universe. The three of us were put on different tables so I wasn't with anyone I really knew. It was quite difficult to see my fellow guests through the terrible table centres – huge glass tubes full of strawberries that had been sort of squished. Smears of red juice everywhere made me think of *CSI* all night!

By the way, did you know that the 'mange tout' is not really a vegetable, but a fruit? I do – well at least I do now – there was a fruit and veg aficionado at our table. I yawned my way through the starter.

Then they did that really awful 'second course shift' thing. All the 'girls' had to move. You know the drill – you end up sitting with another group of eaters, presumably to ensure that you mix with as many people as possible . . . a sort of culinary speed dating. And there is no guarantee the cutlery is clean!

Table two was worse. I'm not sure how they wangled it because I know for sure that I was playing the game right, but for some reason there appeared to be only two SINGLES at this table – me and one other diner. Everyone else had either got lucky really quickly in the evening, or it was a horrible conspiracy to put me alongside perhaps one of the rudest men in Christendom.

He looked me up and down, sighed and made some sarcastic comment about the fact that women over 40 really shouldn't attempt to go out and then promptly started chatting up the young girl next to him, much to the annoyance of her obvious would-be boyfriend. I wanted to say something crushing like, 'And I expected to meet a nice Christian man this evening but obviously that's not happened,' but I didn't get an opportunity because he, and everyone else at the table, just ignored me.

By dessert, I'd managed to escape to sit quietly in a dark corner from where I watched the whole evening descend into an alcoholic haze. I have NEVER seen so much alcohol drunk in one short evening. I know I'm a little unusual in my life choices and seen as pretty odd because I choose not to imbibe, but surely we Christians should be above drinking ourselves into an alcoholic stupor? I wondered for one sanctimonious moment if it was because they were Christian in name only . . .

Whatever the nature of the event, I always find it's hilarious to observe gorgeous people with just a little too much wine in them trying to dance with each other on a darkened dance floor while wearing heels that are far too majestic (the girls) and gradually losing their innate politeness and discovering all sorts of interesting places to place their hands (the boys . . . mostly).

But I have to admit it, the entertainment wore off after a while and I felt rather alone. No one asked me to dance. Of course, it might have been because I was tucked away in that dark corner looking rather like an axe-murderer. Even Prince Charming would have had a hard job convincing me to take to the floor.

My lack of dance opportunities might also have had something to do with the fact that I spent most of the latter part of the evening chatting to the bar and kitchen staff out the back – they were escaping to have a smoke; I was just escaping.

They were MUCH more interesting than the Gorgeous Valentine's People. You'll never believe some of the stories I heard while in that poorly lit alley leading off the kitchen. One of the smokers won the lottery ten years ago but wasted it, gambled it and ended up with only enough money to buy his council house and a bright yellow Nissan Micra. He now works as a dish washer in the hotel kitchen.

His wife ran off with a personal trainer she acquired at an awfully posh gym when they still had dough, and he now works nights while looking after the kids in the daytime and occasionally attempting to sneak in some shut-eye.

I decided then and there that I'm not going to moan about my life again!

However, I can't get away from the fact that the evening was really depressing. I've attended quite a few awful evenings/functions/dinners (PR-related and otherwise) but this was probably the very WORST EVER. In my life! Even more grotesque than that awful fancy dress event last New Year.

Even Rev T scored! Yes ... by the end of the evening she was dancing with Father Sean from St Pete's ... OK, so he's a Catholic priest but ... at least she got a dance!

I have absolutely no idea what happened to Leggy Lynda at the end of the night. Last I saw of her was when she had hunted me down in my dark corner bearing an abnormally attractive Latin-looking man on her arm. Her parting words were, 'Hope you don't mind but Jose is taking me home!'

I know. I know. I know what you're going to say – I shouldn't let this one evening put me off socializing. I really should try to get out and meet people. But last night has decided it for me.

No more singles events for me. If EVER you see me wavering, please, please, please get a wet fish and slap me round the face with it! That's what friends are for!

Esther

DATE: 6 FEBRUARY

✉ Dear E

I had just sat down for a rest with a cup of chai in between opening the door to a procession of sporty teenagers in a variety of muddy sports gear headed by the worst one of them all – Active Jack. They

were soon falling about laughing at your retelling of the singles
Valentine's ball.

Maybe I shouldn't call it a 'ball' as it doesn't sound like you
had one. These are events that we do not know how to do well. I'm
convinced of that now. I think they really give Christianity a bad
name. We both know it is soooo much better than that!

I do know people who have met through Christian 'dating
agencies' or at house parties but you have to wade through a load of
dweebs to find someone interesting. So the question has to be – is
it worth it? I suppose you are showing God you are serious, putting
your foot in a door and hoping that it may open to Mr Right. But it's
not for everyone.

How much were the tickets? I bet they cost a bomb.

Don't get disheartened, though. Maybe we should try doing our
own events – with your PR knowledge and my catering expertise we
could do something a little more interesting and helpful. Couldn't
we? There must be a market for it, if what you say about these
pathetic efforts is anything to go by.

We could make some money (yes the old finances are down in the
dumps once more) and maybe (you anyway – I've obviously got one)
meet a suitable man?

Are you still free on Saturday? Shall we meet at 10 a.m. for
breakfast before we hit the shops? I've got to take the boys out first
thing as they have another football tournament. You would think that Mr
Fitness Fanatic could do it, but no such luck. Thankfully this time I don't
have to stay! Standing on the touchlines midwinter while your beloved
(not so) little ones run around assorted pitches trying to annihilate various
sets of opposition is no longer my idea of a great morning out. This
weekend, I've been given permission to just drop them off. I wonder if
it's because last time I embarrassed Ollie by insisting on checking that he
was wearing his vest and 'lucky' pants? Who knows?

Anyway, shops it is. Haven't got much to get . . . just a Valentine's
card and present for Jack. Just what you don't want to hear! Really
not sure what to get him – I was thinking of the *OO7* DVD box set.
He might like that.

By the way, what did you think of Sam the Boiler Man? He fixed our church heating (sooo glad it's fixed) and I've always thought he's a bit 'hot' (don't tell Jack).

Sam comes highly recommended – for his plumbing ability!

Louise

📧 Hiya Lou

Can we meet at 10.15 please? Have to swill out my smalls (and more) before I take in some retail therapy. Washing machine is now on the blink.

Not really sure what I thought of Sam – I did spend an hour or two with him but most of that time he had his head in my boiler cupboard. He does have a very nice hairline and a good set of shoulders though!

I'll give him credit for something else as well . . . he WAS able to stomach one of my famous BLTs . . . and we didn't have to call the ambulance, so that was good.

Do you think he fixes washing machines too?

E

✉ Hi again Esther

I thought you'd like to know that when I saw Sam in church on Sunday he said you were very friendly and was surprised he hadn't had a chance to really meet or get to know you before. Considering you have come to quite a few social events at our church over the years, it is a surprise. Maybe it is because you've been 'attached' for a couple of years, so there's been no need to check out any available males.

On the subject of church – if you and Sam get friendlier maybe at some point you will finally see the light and shift allegiance. Ours isn't called 'Hope & Light' for nothing.☺

(FYI Sam also runs the New Members group. Isn't that enough to convince you? Only joking!)

He DID mention the snack and I thought was very polite . . . he is very polite.

But seriously E . . . I can't believe that you forced one of your BLTs on him. Can you remember what my boys call them . . . BTB . . . Bacon Totally Burnt?!

You're a brave woman!

Lou

✉ Hi Lou

Rev T would be gutted – I can't shift churches. I need to continue paddling along with Rivers of Life! Plus . . . who else could she drag along to ridiculous singles evenings if not me?

Jokes aside, actually I do think it's a bit early for any new relationship for me, given my current heart condition . . . a bit too soon, post Tom.

On the subject of the BTB, I did offer Sam a free indigestion tablet when I noticed him clutching his chest and stomach but he said he thought the dyspepsia was just the result of crouching down in the boiler cupboard.

You're right . . . he is VERY polite!

E

2

SUBJECT: DEPRESSING DAY

DATE: 15 FEBRUARY

Hi Louise

Hope you're having a great time on your Valentine's mini-break. I can't believe Jack actually managed to surprise you! Long time since that happened. Love you guys. ☺

Is there a pool? Are you having lots of special treats? Hope to hear all about it when you return. Feeling a little jealous — could do with a break.

I guess you may not read this until you get back, but had to vent as it's not been a brilliant couple of days for me all round.

Yesterday I returned home, dog tired at the end of another LONG twelve hours in the office. I know it's my own fault, that's what comes of being a business owner/manager. But some days are more stressful than others.

My two account managers, who both have young kids, both failed to materialize this morning — one on the basis that one of her children had some weird rash and the other giving an excuse that the school was closed due to some unfortunate flooding problem and she couldn't find childcare at such short notice.

I tried to 'Google' which school that might have been (is that terrible, that I just didn't believe her?) but the upshot was — I had to do the work of three today. I just don't know what I would have done without the wonderful Colin. What a find he was! He jumped in with some of the account work and was absolutely fabulous. I've decided I'm going to ensure he learns more of the trade – he's much more than an assistant.

Passing thought here – both the account managers are married, so why is it that when the kids are sick or can't go to school for some reason it's they who have to take the day off? Why not their husbands? Is it social convention? Or are the dads just useless in a crisis? I don't know. I'm baffled. You tell me why – you're the married one.

Anyway, I got home to face yet another microwave dinner, and I found two envelopes on my doormat. I usually love getting post, the real kind where you can feel the paper and smell the ink . . . so unusual these days where it's all email and Twitter and the like . . . not to say I don't enjoy our 'conversations' on email . . . but . . . where was I? Oh yes, the post.

Both envelopes were wedding invitations!

I could tell what the first one was without even opening it. It had that 'joyful announcement' feel about it – embossed envelope and fancy calligraphy instead of the usual ballpoint scrawl.

Don't get me wrong. I know engagements and weddings are a time of rejoicing . . . blah blah blah . . . that's why I feel slightly guilty for feeling depressed. And of course I am thrilled to be invited to an impending nuptial or two. I think.

But as I opened that first envelope my heart sank.

Of course, it's wonderful that Sue and Ron are getting married. They're in my house group and got together (eventually) about two months ago after what seems like years of dancing around each other and smiling quietly across Bibles. It's been obvious to all of us for yonks that Sue has had her eye on him – she always sought him out to be her 'prayer partner' when we did that 'find someone to pray with' point in an evening. But Ron himself has been a bit slower to realize God's purpose for them both!

However, at long last, it happened. I understand their first 'date' was to that Christian counselling weekend . . . very romantic . . . And now, after just two months dating, they're GETTING MARRIED!

What's all THAT about?

This first invitation was actually to Sue and Ron's engagement party. It's next week and they're combining it with house group. Nice.

Now to the second invitation and this one cut the deepest. It was from my old friend Penelope, from school. When was the last time you saw her? At my house, I think, a couple of summers ago when we had that barbecue, the one where Jack burnt all the sausages?

Well anyway, she's getting married shortly – again! This will be her third husband.

Again, I shout out loud:

'WHAT'S ALL THAT ABOUT?'

God won't point me in the direction of even ONE decent potential mate and Penelope is about to hitch herself to a third!

OK, so as you know, her first husband died – I'll give her that. Actually very sad. But . . . three?!

I WANT to be happy for Penny, I really do. After all, at our all-girls' school we shared many anguished moments of 'will I ever find Mr Right?' and 'will anyone ever love me?' I want to feel ecstatic for her. As Christians isn't that what we're meant to be – happy and supportive? I do try. I pray for the grace to override my own problems and help to make a better world. But, sad to say, I have to admit my reaction when opening her envelope was a little less than Christ-like!

First, anger at the injustice of it all. Second, a fleeting moment when I noted that she hadn't bothered with fancy calligraphy – hers was a rather rushed and uninteresting sheet of A4 printed out from the computer. Third reaction – sheer despair and self-pity.

NOW, of course, I feel terribly guilty about my reactions. How's that for a record? Two letters both of which made ME feel guilty? And, of course, I'll attend both functions and smile for everyone, including the cameras. But I'll still be dying inside.

Any advice on dealing with such hideous emotions would be gratefully received, along with any fashion tips. The thought of two new outfits this year is a bit scary, given the state of my bank balance at the moment, post-Christmas and all that – you'll understand, I know.

OK, so the two weddings should (hopefully) not involve the same people, which means I might get away with just one set of new clothes. But is that a bit mean?

You've got loads of experience saving pennies and still managing to look fantastic and I'm urgently in need of help. You know I'm great when it comes to picking out business attire – easy really . . . smart suit, clean shirt and good shoes. I'm even fine with the casual stuff – jeans and crisp T-shirts, trainers and a nice colourful jacket. It's the 'smart/casual' and the 'dressed up' looks that I struggle with. If we need another shopping trip to get me sorted, I'll buy coffee. Or even lunch. I'm glad I still have vouchers left over from Christmas. There's bound to be a sale on somewhere.

So that's my moaning Minnie impression over. Again, hope you're having a wonderfully romantic time . . . you lucky old thing!

God bless

Esther

✉ Hi Esther

I opened your email sitting here in my lovely hotel suite, surrounded by flowers and chocolates . . . Jack's way of saying 'sorry', I guess, for spending most of our 'romantic break' in the ever-so-impressive resort gym.

It IS a marvellous facility! He dragged me down there in great excitement on our first evening to point out the various pieces of equipment he was planning on trying out during our stay. The running machine is like something from outer space – all computerized with lots of flashing lights and buzzers! There are weights and rowing machines and a sort of souped-up exercise bike that is for something called 'Spinning'.

If I'd have wanted to 'Spin' I'd have gone to that evening class to learn how to make my own woollen clothing, or asked my mum. She actually is a great spinner!

Anyway, I was livid!

But then I looked at Jack's face and he was glowing with excitement. He really had no idea at all that I might feel slightly cheated at the prospect of my husband spending more time in the gym than with me during out 'romantic interlude'. My anger subsided slightly but I felt I did have to explain, as calmly as possible, that my idea of a 'mini-break' involved a little more than sitting watching him sweat for England, and rubbing his aching legs (now that's something you really don't want to know much about!).

In the distant past, he might have said, 'Well you could always join me in the gym,' but I think, after nineteen years of marital bliss, he knows better. So we came to a mutual understanding. We've had some great walks in the lovely countryside, and some wonderful meals. Last night we attended a 'dance' in the hotel (in the old days I would have called it a disco but we're a little more sophisticated now) and I managed to drag Jack onto the floor a couple of times, despite his protestations of 'I can't dance! My calves hurt!' He goes off to the gym in the mornings and again in the late afternoon. I lounge by the pool and do a few things like answer emails and read. You know me: I'd rather catch up with a good book than expose myself to strangers. However, am regretting now that I never did get a new costume and matching wrap. I'm catching up with a lot of books. I have also managed a jazz dance class, which was great fun although I fear I will never feature on the West End stage.

I'm home on Tuesday and hoping not to return to Armageddon. I am glad that Jack persuaded his sister Charise to come by and look after the boys while we are away, but they always run rings around her – she's just too sweet!

Now, onto the subject of weddings!

You know what I think about it all. You either go to the ceremony and endure it, or miss it and do something else and risk offending the inviters. There are no easy answers but there are plenty of other things you can do with your weekends off. How about doing one of those intensive 'basic cooking' courses? There are some really good ones around. You could learn to fly, go rally driving or 'sphereing'.

Despite my lack of interest in the gym, I have always fancied the latter but Jack says that rolling down hills in a big plastic ball is for hamsters not church elders' wives. One day I will prove him wrong. ☺ I really can't understand his reaction given the amount of time he spends each week on a treadmill!

I can't believe Penelope is marrying again! What's he like? Have I met him? She obviously feels that she can't remain in an unmarried state. No wonder it was a cheap invite – weddings cost a bomb.

Maybe they should apply for that programme *Don't Tell the Bride*. What kind of wedding would her fiancé organize with £1,200, bearing in mind her first wedding was in St Lucia and the second in the Scottish castle that Madonna was married in?

Jack has just come in exhausted from a gym session – it's our last night here tonight but I am suspecting that he'll be snoring by 9 p.m. Oh well; that's married life for you!

However, he does have some suggestions for Penny's next nuptial. Underwater wedding – she loves the sea and the sun, doesn't she? The bride wore flippers? Or how about a theatre-themed wedding since she's such a drama queen? Or what about *Pirates of the Caribbean* – isn't her surname Knightly? Has she got a sister called Keira?

I think the world should introduce a new wedding rule. Anyone who wants you to come to their special day and expects their guests to wear new outfits should pay up. It costs a fortune these days to attend a wedding: new clothes, present, getting there, accommodation where necessary, etc. I love attending weddings but they are so expensive. I wonder if they were so expensive in the past . . .

We have a couple in our church who will have been married sixty years this year. What a fantastic example of love and commitment. If you ask them what has held them together they say they have several golden rules. 1. Never go to bed on an argument. 2. Give and take. 3. Remember, neither of you are perfect but God is still working on you. 4. Treats . . . spoil each other from time to time. But what they say is really the foundation of their relationship is their shared love of Jesus. His love means they can love each other even when at times they don't like each other. At first, I thought that was strange but I now know what they mean. There are moments when I do not like Jack – when he disappears to the gym on our romantic weekend, for example – but I do love him.

So, enough mushy stuff, until they change the rules on wedding outfits, I may have something you can borrow but very happy to go shopping again to escape all things male at my house. When I get home and I've sorted out the mess I'm sure to find I will need some time out. This little break has gone some way to helping me feel not so much like a drowning woman, but I still feel a bit lost. Jack is so caught up in this big work project he has going on and of course he's training for the half-marathon. He also has that major presentation in Amsterdam looming large. I'm still narked that I wasn't invited to accompany him as I have never been to Anne Frank's house.

I know I should be grateful to God that I have healthy children and a fit husband but sometimes the grass is greener on the other side. Which reminds me, when I get home I've got that big cupcake order to fill – you know, the one with lime green frosting!

Who orders green frosting for a retirement 'do'? That is the question.

Louise

DATE: 16 FEBRUARY

⌨ Dear Lou

Sounds like a Hulk order not a bulk order. Keep smiling! ☺

Sorry I went on a bit before – I do need to remind myself every so often that it's not all about me and my feelings. Others are also struggling through life as well. Remember you can always offload on me. That's what friends are for. If you want help doing that green frosting let me know. Don't try and do it all alone! I won't know what I'm doing, you know that – but happy to help with mixing and stirring under supervision, so long as I don't have to do anything too technical.

As for Penelope's new man, his name is Clive and I think he might be a bit well off so *Don't Tell the Bride* can breathe a sigh of relief, although that would have made excellent viewing!

And, no, you haven't met him. In fact I haven't met him! I don't even know how they met. I'm sure she will fill in all the details with twinkling bells and sparkly things!

E xx

PS Basic cooking course? Are you telling me I can't acquit myself in the kitchen? What about that dish I brought round for you guys when you were all a bit unwell last October? Are you saying that Duck a l'Orange curry didn't help you all feel just a little bit better?

PPS You don't want me to write a piece about your amazing couple for the local rag, do you? Free PR for the church? Get their permission, obviously. Ask your Rev.

DATE: 19 FEBRUARY

Dear Louise

Do you still have that box of chocolates from your mini-break? If so, can you bring it round this afternoon please? I'm in desperate need of strawberry creams or a nougat-centred something. So long as none of the sweeties are heart-shaped with cherry stuff in the middle. Yuk on both counts!

You'll never guess what happened at church this morning. I got attacked by the loved-up Sue and Ron, who bounded over to me after the family service.

They've set the wedding date – the invitation is apparently in the post. Another calligraphy masterpiece no doubt, she is one of those 'creative' people who makes everything from scratch. Some of it is good recycling but some of her efforts just look plain weird. Her recent Christmas card was an odd mixture of crafty bits – Jesus in the manager, a lovely star and Father Christmas coming over the hill. Not a patch on your fantastic card creations!

But it's not the invitation I'm dreading. What really shocked me is the date they've chosen – 16 September.

Can you believe it? I couldn't!

'We were so fortunate,' Sue gushed at me. 'The church had a cancellation!'

They desperately wanted that day; apparently it's Ron birthday and that means 'he won't EVER forget our wedding day!' so they were thrilled to get it.

As you can imagine, I was so GUTTED I nearly fell over.

I certainly couldn't open my mouth to tell her that I knew that Rivers of Life had a cancellation on 16 September. That day is circled in my diary as MY wedding day. I wanted to scream at them that it was ME who had cancelled and left the day conveniently open for them!

But it gets worse. After the first revelation, Sue cornered me privately in the vestibule and . . . get this . . . asked if she might 'borrow' my wedding dress!

'I know you were getting married and aren't now, and I just can't find the right dress but Anne says she knows YOURS was lovely so if you've still got it and don't mind, I wondered if I might . . . you know . . .'

Apparently they're a bit short of cash (buying a three-bedroomed house with a view to filling it very soon with lots of babies) so she doesn't even want to buy it. She rambled on: 'No use to you now, we're friends, etc.'

She's asked to come round mine after tonight's evening fellowship to give it the once over and try it on, although she's already warned me that, what with the cabbage soup diet, she'll probably have to have it taken in several sizes! And as 'white doesn't really suit me', she's hinted that she might like to dye it slightly cream! She is a bit wacky with her dress sense, lots of tie-dye skirts . . . but . . . I feel a bit nauseous at the thought.

I was so speechless (yes, I know it's hard to believe) and I don't think I put her off. So if you can come round with the chocs, you'll just happen to be here for a bit of moral support if she does pitch up. Tried to ring, but Ollie must be on the phone again. Is it still that

Chloe girl or have his affections moved on? Anyway, sorry for the short notice but ... HELP!!

E

✉ Esther

I just read the email and re-read it – twice. So sorry I was not available – or there for you. Our phones are used a lot. You should have rung the mobile. I do answer it sometimes!
How can Sue be so insensitive?

You are so kind – just say 'NO'! Next, she will be asking for the matching veil and shoes. I would like to be there when she comes round. I am very good at providing a slap in love. I told Jack and he just stomped around growling like a dog and muttering stuff like, 'there are some mad Christians'.

Signing off, one angry

Louise

✉ Dear Esther

Hope you don't mind but I have interfered a bit and just picked up the phone to Sue. I had her number because she is the one who ordered the lime green cupcakes for a colleague's recent 'leaving do' ...

Don't worry, I didn't pop her heart-shaped bubble completely, but I reminded her that her wedding dress request was a bit insensitive. The fact that she doesn't know me that well helped. I also caught her mid-lunch and she sounded like she had a mouthful of roast. Don't you just HATE that ... when people ring during meal times? Oops! ☺

I do think she was a little surprised that I knew about your conversation but I explained, saying something like, 'As you know, Esther and I have known each other for years and share all our most traumatic experiences.'

I reminded her of the significance of 16 September and she was, admittedly, a bit shocked. I really don't think she had put two and two together – cancelled wedding/free date/spare wedding dress hanging in your wardrobe. I can't believe she forgot – wasn't she originally invited to your and Tom's wedding?

Once I was on a roll, I'm afraid I didn't leave it there. I ploughed in about the insensitivity of the dress issue. Why did she think you had an available white dress in the first place? She muttered something about whether it would 'jinx' their day, which didn't sound very Christian to me. The conversation ended shortly afterwards.

Hope I haven't put my foot in it.

Lou xx

 Just got back from evening fellowship – Sue wasn't there. Yikes. I guess she didn't want to face me! Thanks though – should've been braver and stood up for myself. The heart still hurts! Don't think indigestion tablets help this kind of pain. Any suggestions? E

 God will ease the pain but it is a loss like a bereavement. Give yourself time. The waves of grief will ease and one day you may even see Tom or go to a wedding without asking the question, 'What if?' Louise xxx

DATE: 20 FEBRUARY

⌨ Dear L

Thank you for being a great friend, as always. You're right. I'm bound to have good and bad days but yesterday was a humdinger. I just want to feel normal again.

Now back to interviewing. Got a vacancy to fill here.

E

✉ Dear Esther

You are normal – will I regret saying that?

   I do hope the vacancy is a work post not a man post?! Be gentle with yourself and give yourself time to be content as you. You are a fantastic friend and I thank God for our friendship. He has blessed us with so much. Will keep praying.

Lou x

DATE: 21 FEBRUARY

🗎 Hi Lou

The vacancy is for a new account manager – one of the marrieds decided after the last offspring emergency incident that she needed to spend more time with the family. Bit sad really – one of her children was recently diagnosed with a mild form of autism.

   Is it just me or is this becoming more and more common? Or maybe it's just because it's being picked up now and recognized by the medical profession? I remember there was a boy in my class at junior school and he was always considered a little bit 'odd' by the rest of us, because he wouldn't speak much and spent a lot of time by the fence in the playground. I always felt really sorry for him because he had hardly any friends, but it was about the age when to be 'buddies' with a boy, or even to be seen speaking to a boy, was not considered quite the thing . . . you know, the lads were all about 'girls' fleas' and we steered clear of 'boys' fleas'.

   Anyway, my colleague's little girl was recently diagnosed and so she's decided she needs to be at home. Probably a good decision given that the little lass will need some extra help.

E

✉ Hi Esther

Hope you get the right replacement! It's sad to hear about your
account manager's little girl. I know how hard it was to juggle work
and three little boys, and none of mine had special needs.

I am currently running around trying to complete orders while
praying for more. It's mad, I know, when I am so busy that I just
about manage to fulfil the orders I do have, that I need more to make
ends meet. It's this economic climate – bad for small businesses.

You don't fancy helping a friend do some baking, do you? I
promise I will supervise. I know you said your last cupcake effort
resembled something that might just about pass off as pancakes. I've
told you . . . if you need cake, just ask. And if I ever need Duck a
l'Orange curry, I will know where to come.

By the way, I don't think I told you but when Jack and I returned
from our lovely romantic mini-break, the house was in good
condition. At least, that's what we thought. Everything in its place,
clean and tidy, no breakages. We were very impressed. Charise had, it
appeared, managed to retain a modicum of control over the household.

That night we sat down to watch some TV and have a cuddle
on the sofa, still glowing with pride that our boys had managed to
behave so impeccably over a whole weekend.

It was when Jack turned to me and said, 'Is it just me, or are my
legs longer than they were when we left for the resort?' that we
realized that the sofa was nearer to the floor than it used to be. Jack's
legs had not, magically, grown over a long weekend of vigorous
exercise (in the gym). The sofa had lost its legs!

In fact, when we examined the piece of furniture, we discovered
that there were now four bricks where the legs used to be.

The boys were out – we'd given them all extra pocket money for
their 'good behaviour' and they had gone to the cinema – so we had to
wait a while to discover what had happened to our previously perfect
couch. It was hard to keep calm and collected awaiting their return.

We have since discovered that on the Friday night, barely hours
after we had left home, the boys and several of their friends who,

unbeknown to us, they had invited around for pizza, decided to use our lovely living room furniture as a trampoline. One bounce too many and the cross bar of the sofa snapped and the legs splayed and broke. We have a carpenter coming tomorrow to examine the damage. But meanwhile we've propped the couch up with loads of Jack's books – he's not that happy and neither are the boys because they now have to sit on the floor to watch telly.

I know you want to know . . . where was Charise in all this? She was enjoying a lovely bubble bath in my en suite and the boys did such a great (and rapid) job of hiding the evidence of their sins, that she never even noticed the legless sofa!

Kids – who would have them?

Lou xxx

DATE: 22 FEBRUARY

✉ Dear Esther

Under conviction – just watched a programme on the TV mentioning how a lot of small businesses have had to close and it's made me realize how much I have to be thankful for.

God has been good, and, despite the ups and downs, my little business is still afloat. I am not having to resort to food banks to feed my family, and Jack's work is picking up tremendously. All we need now is for his cheques to be in the bank in time to help settle the ever-growing mound of household bills. As you know, when I started Lou's Cupcakes I promised never to steal from the household account to pay for the business. It's been close some months, but I've always managed it. However, it seems like the moment I get ahead of myself another bill crops up and puts me back to square one.

I know I moan a lot about money but it's just so worrying. The other night I found myself sitting in the kitchen drinking tea at 3.20 a.m. – Jack came down to find me. I was sitting there with a piece of paper trying to work out something or other. When he asked me what I was doing, for the life of me I could not remember. It was THAT important!

Lou

✉ Dear Lou

Don't worry. I know that's easy to say, but it really doesn't get us anywhere when we worry about things which might never happen. What is it the Bible says? Something like, 'Consider the lilies of the field. They do not labour or spin . . .' Bit strange, but I think what it means is we do not need to worry about life. Keep your focus on the things that matter. It's a tough one.

   If I can help in any way, let me know. Wish I'd seen that programme – you didn't happen to record it did you?

E xx

✉ Dear Esther

The programme was called something like *Backfiring Businesses* . . . it should be on Watch Again.

L xxx

3

SUBJECT: I AM A WOMAN!

DATE: 24 FEBRUARY

✉ Dear Esther

After you left the other night I remembered I didn't tell you about what happened when I went with Jacqui to church. It was a really funny incident but exasperating in other ways. Not an example to be included in the *Welcome People and Introduce Them to Church Manual*! We have a fantastic welcome team at Hope & Light, and I cannot imagine them ever doing this. Makes me mad just to think about it.

You may remember Jacqui – she makes fab cupcakes and I employ her for the larger orders? I actually met her through a Christians in Cake group . . . Yes, there IS such a thing. She helped me with Sue's hideous lime green order the other week!

She used to live about an hour away but has been exploring this area a bit since she started doing some work for me, and decided to move house. She was a bit nervous about going to a new church alone so I said I would go with her. I did try to persuade her to come to Hope & Light but it's not really her thing . . . she's a bit more happy clappy than that and, anyway, she wanted a church within walking distance of her new flat.

So Sunday morning I drove over to the church she'd identified as one where she might fit in. We thought we were just about 'on time' but when we arrived we realized that the service started at 11.30, not on the hour – they had just added a morning service for the Spring (is it Spring yet? Could have fooled me – did you see that frost the other morning?). Anyway, the time of the second family service was different to that advertised.

We were sitting outside – yes in the freezing cold – as we didn't want to go in too early, and this younger woman turned up. We chatted – she's called Suzie. She's interested in God, although not a Christian. She'd had a hard few months and wondered if God was interested in her. That morning she had woken up and thought 'maybe I should go to church'. Isn't that wonderful? It's amazing what God does in quiet moments. And there she was, standing in front of us.

We shared what God means to us and even prayed with her. What a privilege. It was really cool (in every respect).

Then we all went in to the church service, which was OK. A lot of singing the same song twenty times kind of place. To be honest, judging from her initial reaction, I'm not sure Jacqui will settle there but she's giving it a go.

After the service there was coffee and tea and dry biscuits and I, particularly, was keen to try to see if there was someone from the church who might take Suzie under their wing and maybe explain about the services and what happens at the church. Jacqui was off chatting to one of the elders – I could see her out of the corner of my eye trying to fend off a man in a tweed jacket who was waving some leaflets.

I spotted the bloke who had led the service and thought, 'He must be the minister . . . I'll get him to speak to Suzie.' I explained the situation to him, expecting him to immediately say, 'Thank you SO MUCH! Let me meet her!'

However, instead, he looked at me as if I was an alien from another planet and pronounced, 'You are a woman and I am a man – let me get my wife!'

Well you know me – I was not impressed. I returned to Suzie and drank lukewarm tea for ten minutes. No one appeared, so I hunted down someone else who was also obviously a leader . . . interesting how you can spot they are a church leader so easily, isn't it? They don't really have any distinguishing signs but it sort of oozes out of them!

By then I was getting stressed because I needed to head home to see Jack and co. Jack was heading off early Monday morning and I wanted to spend some time with him.

Anyway, the conversation went something like this. I explained that Suzie was a young woman seeking something spiritual; God had spoken to her that morning, even if she didn't know it yet.

The (second) man (hope you're keeping up) looked at me and frowned slightly. Without giving him a chance to open his mouth, I jumped in: 'Before you say anything – yes I am a woman and you are a man but this lady wants to know Jesus and wants to come to your church. Please speak to her, welcome her and give her a Bible. Chat to her about Jesus who loves us and tell her about your Alpha course but don't make her wait any longer because she is a woman and you are a man!'

Bless him – after speaking to Scary Woman he did do just that. Although I prayed all the way home for Suzie I'm not sure really. It seemed like a friendly church but at the end of the day if their leaders think that only a woman can talk to a woman about Jesus, and a man to a man, then we're in trouble.

As I say, I'm not sure Jacqui will stay. It is such a shame.

Lou x

📧 Dear Lou

Well done you! 1. For getting up the courage to 'witness' to Suzie in such a bold way and 2. For praying with her! That's so you. That's how we should be sharing our faith, just naturally in conversation, friendly and without any sort of embarrassment. No preaching, just talking about our life with Jesus.

And well done for tackling the awful authorities. I know we are called to respect our leaders but occasionally things are not right. There are so many great leaders but these sound positively Neanderthal in their approach to evangelism.

What are they thinking? How on earth will we grow churches when we've such a 'them and us' attitude, and when there is such sexist weirdness inside church? Jesus is the most inclusive person I know!

Their reaction was the absolute opposite of what you did on their doorstep. Maybe that's where we should 'do church'.

OK, so I know lots and lots of our fellow churchgoers believe that those of us without you know what between our legs are MEANT to stay quiet in the corner with our heads covered but really . . .

Anyway, if I were Jacqui I wouldn't want to stay there – not unless she wants to permanently sit at the back (or do they still have different sections for women?) and be resigned to making the coffee and tea if the elders deem her worthy. Maybe that's why the beverages were so awful . . . the only way the women can fight back? Revolution through the refreshments?

It's a shame Jacqui can't travel the distance to get a little Hope & Light. Can't you persuade her? Alternatively, she might like to try Rivers of Life. Either way, we're sure to be able to help her find a church that will suit her, wherever it's geographically situated.

And did you get Suzie's details at all? Perhaps we should invite her to the girls' night out next month and let her see that us Christians are not weird aliens after all but just normal . . . well . . . almost.

E

PS See you at the cheese and wine affair at Rivers tomorrow?

DATE: 28 FEBRUARY

✉ Dear E

I am looking forward to our girls' night out but I may need to do some Suzie repair work before extending an invitation. I am praying that she did not hear any of my conversations with the awful leaders – but if she did we're scuppered. Church can be so wonderful. We both know what God has done for us but as his people we do step in sometimes and make a mess of things. Praying the truth will shine through the appalling incident.

So to help, here is a suggestion. As well as the girls' night out maybe we can invite Suzie to a 'mixed' dinner party. She needs to know that we are all made in God's image – men and women – and that we are equal in his sight.

I also think it would be good for Suzie to see that Christians come in all shapes and sizes – appropriate because at the moment I feel like the size of a small Eastern European nation. I really MUST stop sampling the cupcakes – although someone needs to taste them. Maybe I need to think about the gym. Jack would be pleased. One year for my birthday he bought me gym gear. It upset me at the time – yes, I shouted: 'DO YOU THINK I AM FAT?' – but his heart was in the right place!

Jack was mad when I told him about the incident, not the eating cupcakes but about what happened at Jacqui's church. We are praying for Suzie.

L

✉ Dear Lou

Dinner party is a good idea but PLEASE can we make sure that it's not just established couples and a few odd males and females scattered around?

Although it might work for Suzie (if she has a partner) it's not so great for invited singles.

When I was with Tom (gritted teeth) I didn't mind these events at all although I still had a vague memory of what it was like BEFORE, when I would turn up at parties only to find that there were six couples and four 'spares' – conveniently two male and two female and . . . oh what a coincidence . . . we were sitting next to each other. OK if you've been warned in advance but not so great if it's a 'surprise'!

NOW, of course, I'm back to that again, although as chance would have it I've not yet been invited to any parties as a 'newly single'. Maybe

Life Lines

it's because people feel awkward about my 'situation' or maybe some of the women feel I might throw myself at their 'other halves'.

I know I'm ultra-sensitive about this but, instead of a formal dinner party, how about an 'open house' evening where we can be sure to invite lots of random people and it might not seem so obvious to the singles that they are in a minority?

E

✉ Dear E

You are not being sensitive. We all face our battles with roles and identity.

Did I never tell you about the trip we made to Sheffield when the kids were small? Jack was preaching at a church there back in the days when he had time to preach, and he delivered a great sermon that morning. Don't ask me what it was – I just know it fed me!

After the service a loud, tall American gentleman approached me. 'You must be so proud of him,' he said to me, towering from above. Then, while I was trying to nod in agreement, he went on, 'So what do you do, lovely lady? I suppose you stay at home looking after these little ones?'

Forgetting where I was I replied, 'No, I write his sermons for him,' and walked off, leaving the gentleman to regain his posture and pick up his jaw.

I struggle with who people think I am at times. And I think we can assume that if someone is single we are doing them a favour inviting them to a dinner party with at least one other nominal singleton. It is just like people assuming that all 'marrieds' are happy in the traditional role of 'husband' and 'wife' which, if truth be told, is far from reality these days.

Must go. Laurence came home last night with a bloody knee – a football injury, of course – and, although I gagged, I managed to clean it up. Today, however, it's looking pretty sore so we're off to

A&E to have it poked by a nurse. Although he's trying to be brave he is in pain. And although he's 13, he's still my baby!

Lou x

⬜ Hi Lou

You should have said, 'Actually I'm the pastor at our church and Jack helps me out.' Now THAT would have shocked him! But don't get me started on women priests, vicars and leaders ... we'd be here until midnight!

Esther xxx

PS Love to Laurence. Ouch!

4

SUBJECT: TOO FUSSY?

DATE: 2 MARCH

Hi Louise

It was SO good to see you at last Saturday's Rivers of Life cheese and wine affair and I forgot to say thanks again for rescuing me from the guy with the fold-over hair and the beige sweater and bright green tie.

I'm know I'm single now, but really – why does that mean I'm a magnet for every weird chap in my church and, apparently, every other congregation in the district? It's like the word has gone round: 'ESTHER IS NOW AVAILABLE!'

Just last weekend some random chap, who I think goes to St Pete's, stopped me in the street and after first asking me if I was alright, wondered if I might like to drop in to the café at Wendleworth's to share a cup of tea. I don't even know his name. I politely declined . . .

Am I too fussy? That is the question!

Right now, coming off the back of the break-up, I waver between feeling like I'm on the shelf, discarded and desperate enough to consider hooking up with just about any male that crosses my path and is still able to stand on his own two feet – if only to prevent me being jumped on by total strangers – to resolutely determining on forever virginity, well at least until God points me in the direction of The One. Again.

The problem is, time is moving swiftly on and it doesn't look like God is up for any kind of revelation on the husband front any time soon.

However, I am beginning to wonder if soon the only eligible men will be widowed or divorced ... or those frankly odd ones I've previously described!

I told you how Angela 'shared in love' with me the other Sunday over after-church tea and coffee in the foyer? Yes, apparently God has spoken to her and hubbie Geoff about this but not to me directly, so it was up to Angela to share the message – God means me to be single, and remain celibate, for the good of the Kingdom!

I get that a lot. All from very well-meaning people who have no idea how much it hurts me.

So, as my only married Christian friend who is even halfway 'normal' and with any sense of reality, what do you reckon to my 'situation'?

Esther

PS I know you'll recommend 'praying about it' but just so you know I do that already. A lot. A LOT! I even fast occasionally.

PPS Maybe the best decision is to realize that the whole thing is entirely ridiculous, it's only society that tells us we're worthless unless we're married, and that I really am better off on my own after all? Maybe that IS God's plan for me? Maybe Angela is right?!

✉ Hi E

Yes, the cheese and wine guy definitely needs to meet Gok Wan! Fold-over hair is sooo last year!

I am afraid it's people's fault that you get put in these situations. We do not always act as God wants. There is such an emphasis, especially in church, that attaining the state of marriage is something we all need not just to aspire to, but achieve.

I'm coming to the conclusion that it's not necessarily the case. I think part of the answer in life is being content with who you are, in whatever situation God has placed you.

People can be so insensitive. Please tell me if I ever am.

Just remind yourself when the weird people accost you in the street and want to frogmarch you off on a date that you are content as you are for the time being and that, after all, Jesus was single and he's not a bad example!

What was your response to Angela? You didn't say. Did you remind her that you appreciate her 'words' for you but that God does speak to you directly too, and if he wanted to tell you that you need to resign yourself to perpetual singleness perhaps he would not wish the news to be broken to you over a lukewarm cup of sweet tea in a noisy church foyer?

I firmly believe that God wants to place us in families and that he does give us the desire of our hearts. When and where would be nice to know! I admire your perseverance and patience!

Just thinking . . . do you think Angela would like to come to my jewellery party?

Louise

DATE: 3 MARCH

🖃 Hi Lou

Don't want to be un-Christian about it but . . . NO NO NO! Please . . . NO!

Ten minutes with the blessed Angela after church is enough. Heaven forbid what would happen to my fixed smile if I had to spend a couple of hours with her in the intimate environment of your front lounge.

Plus, she's one of those ladies who doesn't really 'do' jewellery, apart from her wedding and engagement ring and the gold cross necklace. You know the sort – doesn't believe women should wear trousers or adorn themselves unnecessarily.

She's taken me to task before ('in Christian love' of course) and tackled me on my attire. We were at choir practice once and

I turned up in my multi-coloured ski jacket – you know the one; purple, orange and bright green patches? Well it gets me noticed when I'm upside down in a snowdrift.

I was wearing it that night because 1. It was cold outside and 2. It was even colder inside church because the heating was broken. There was no way I was risking hypothermia while trying to negotiate Handel's 'Messiah'!

Anyway, after choir practice Angela nabbed me and said something like, 'Dear, do we REALLY want to wear such bright outrageous clothing? That's not going to get us a nice young man now is it?'

Isn't it funny how when God is speaking through Angela he speaks in the third person?

Anyway, I was tired and cold, having spent an hour or so trying to share body heat with the other two girls in the alto section – both of whom are so slim I think I lost more warmth than I gained. So I disgraced myself really. Yes my sharp tongue came out. I'm ashamed. I admit it.

I think I replied something along the lines of, 'Thanks for the fashion tip, Angela, but I'm not sure it's valid coming from someone who wears floral skirts in winter. By the way, did you realize your legs are so blue they match your hideous cardie?'

So, please, no jewellery party that includes Angela on the guest list. It's not a great idea if I'm to remain sane. Anyway, for Angela an hour spent in the presence of a dozen or so Jezebels would be tantamount to consorting with Satan himself, even though the party is raising money for a good cause – what is it again?

Poor Old Geoff, I do feel so sorry for him. I can't imagine what it would be like being married to Angela. But then I suppose he knows no better? Did you know she chooses his clothes for him every morning so they wear matching outfits/colours? Angela believes it is so people can see they really complement each other.

What can you say to that?

Esther

DATE: 4 MARCH

📧 Hi Lou

Just remembered I forgot to tell you my reaction to Angela's pronouncement that God means me to be single/celibate.

My knee-jerk reaction would have been something like, 'Thanks, Angela, I'm guessing you and Geoff know all about celibacy,' (the thought of the two of them 'together' is quite weird) but I bit my tongue. I really didn't want to repeat the shameful quick-fire nastiness that followed the ski jacket comment.

Also, I don't think it was a coincidence that just that week I'd read in my daily Bible reading something from Proverbs 15. Verse 11 I think it is: 'A gentle answer turns away wrath, but a harsh word stirs up anger.'

That thought just popped into my head – as you know I'm not usually one for saying, 'God spoke to me,' but it felt a bit like he did.

So, I looked Angela straight in the eye and said, hopefully not TOO sarcastically . . .

'Well thank you Angela. And thank Geoff too, will you? I appreciate your concern. But I hope if God has such a profound message for me, he may communicate it directly.'

How's that?

E

✉ Dear Esther

Well done! Reminds me of that other biblical phrase 'heaping burning coals' on someone's head . . . probably completely out of context but if that didn't make Angela feel a little awkward then I am not sure what will.

I am about to sell some items on eBay and wondered if you wanted me to add your ski jacket? Some poor skier who wants to get noticed on the snowy white alpine slopes may appreciate it rather than blinding a humble driver in leafy suburbia!

Louise

PS Also happy to go shopping with you for a lovely warm fleece lined PLAIN jacket. ☺

PPS Are you going skiing this year or do you have other holiday plans? If you get a tax rebate how about a cruise?

✉ Thanks Lou

Plain fleeces are for sheep! I know you like lambs and bleat on about how cute they are but I say, stand out from the crowd – don't be part of the flock and go for bright and adventurous! At least in your choice of jacket if not in life.

I certainly don't intend to sell my coat of many colours. The Angelas of this world will just have to grin and bear it – and get a life.

Not sure about the holiday situation. I was, of course, looking forward to a fab fortnight in the Maldives (honeymoon) so I'm at a bit of a loss. I might go to visit my aunts and cousins in Canada. Not quite the same, I know, but it could be fun. Haven't seen my mum's family for years and my cousins are always asking when I'm going to visit. Plus my brother-in-law's mob is always willing to put me up.

Still thinking.

E xx

5

SUBJECT: AND A BIT OF SOAP . . .

DATE: 11 MARCH

✉ Hiya Esther

Thanks for your help last night at the jewellery party. We really pulled it together quite quickly, didn't we? I'm thrilled at the £354.64 raised – thanks for making it up to £360. The secretary of Laurence's PTA will be delighted. It was good fun and a great fundraising idea. Wasn't it great to clear out our jewellery boxes and replace the old stock with some new-to-us items at a low cost? We must do it again sometime.

I have to report, however, that Jack is still in shock. He's wandering around the house today looking a little shell-shocked. He just cannot understand why Allegra – the woman from the local flower shop who I invited on the spur of the moment – brought Jason to the party when no one else carted their hubbies along and all Allegra did was drink our nice red wine and it was JASON who was looking (and trying out) the jewellery.

I did always think Jason looked a little camp. Do you think it's deliberate or can he not help it? Maybe it's the bright pink sweater that gives it away, although Allegra swears that it's just part of the golfing gear . . . a golf sweater at a jewellery party? I don't think so!

Anyway, as soon as everyone had gone last night, Jack confided in me that Jason has made what he thought might be a 'romantic advance' towards him, telling him he looked so fit and he thought Jack was the spitting image of Daniel Craig. Did we know that Jason might be the other way inclined? Does Allegra know that her husband might not be the person she thinks he is? It's beginning to sound like a soap opera! Oh relationships . . . they are weird.

Been thinking about divorce and marriage. I think it is because it seems that more and more of our friends are in troubled marriages. It's everywhere – in church and outside church. Did I tell you that a couple from Hope & Light are, sadly, getting divorced after being married for twenty-three years? Bit ironic really – no hope left and it's all a bit dark at the moment for their relationship. James and Catherine – you know them, don't you?

Twenty-three years is more than a life sentence; the hard work is done, but now, it's all over!

I wonder if people don't appreciate the fact that as they get married and time passes they change. They are not the people they were on their wedding day. In my case that is a good thing as I was so airy-fairy. Head in the clouds with so many silly ideas. Now I think I am too practical – sorting out the boys, the house, work, etc. I don't feel I have time to invest in even one half of our marriage. Don't worry – Jack and I are not in trouble – but you do change and you can embrace that in a person and see God changing them for the better, or you can pull against it. That's why a renewal of vows every ten years is a good idea.

Did you know that the common age for the onset time for divorce is when couples hit their 40s? Maybe it's because in their 20s people are in the first flush, then by the time people reach their 30s they just don't have time to think about any problems, usually being up to their eyes in family life and the like. It's when people get to their 40s that they struggle, especially if they have not 'invested' in their marriage. It's then that they have more time to talk, but often don't know where to start. They have often fallen into bad habits, invariably have different interests and have 'grown apart'.

Sorry for going all philosophical! I have just been thinking about it.

Louise

PS I told you that the Marriage Growth course would come in handy one day!

✉ Dear Esther

Me again. I'm in the spirit of all things charitable. I am thinking of doing a sponsored swim for Africa. What do you think?

I was challenged this week during the sermon – do I put God first and at the centre of my life? Sometimes my time with God is squeezed into a two-minute slot between washing, baking, general caretaking and doing all the things a wife and mother has to do. But can I really be a good wife, mother or friend if I don't spend time with my best friend? God-filled moments give me the fuel I need to motor through each day. Helps me to focus on the right things.

I can always tell when my life gets out of spiritual balance – things just become too much for me. Perhaps you can help and tell me when you think I'm going a bit 'off piste' and out of rhythm.

Lou x

PS Should have said sponsored SLIM not swim. Taking to the pool would be just too physical – although Daniel Craig could do the swim and I could do the slim.

DATE: 12 MARCH

🖹 Hi Lou

Got to say I had wondered why Jack looked so pale midway through the jewellery party. Tell him it's a blessing to look like Daniel C, and he certainly looked the part in his tuxedo serving the drinks to us ladies (and Jason). It's better than looking like Dame Edna ... oh, it's just come to me, THAT's who Jason reminds me of!

I think you seem to have a good balance – but, never fear, I will remind you if you are out of focus!

On the James and Catherine front, although I'm certainly no expert in love and marriage I have done a lot of observing from the sidelines and I'm just stunned by their news! They seemed so happy.

Always holding hands and finishing each other's sentences. Just shows you can never tell what goes on behind closed doors. It's a cliché but so true! I feel so sorry for them and their girls.

I want to get in touch with both of them and send them my support, but might that be a bit weird and could it be misinterpreted?

I've told you that I feel like I'm on the open market now that I'm newly single. Well, the same thing happened to my friend Duncan – you know the organist at our church? He told me that when he split from his girlfriend Justine no sooner had word got round the district than he felt like he was up for auction. Every single Christian woman in his world, of all ages, called him, emailed, texted and wanted to be his friend on Facebook. He confided in me – the only female friend he felt safe with – that it made him feel a bit like a piece of meat!

So, although calling Catherine would be safe, making contact with James might be misconstrued? It's difficult.

At least you recognize that things have changed through the years with you and Jack and you're working on it together. Maybe that was James and Catherine's problem? Perhaps they just thought everything would always be the same. I don't know. Who am I to comment? I couldn't even maintain a successful engagement.

Give my love to OO7. And tell him not to worry about Jason, but that he might want to avoid going into the flower shop for a while.

E x

6

SUBJECT: THOUGHTS ON ST PAUL

DATE: 15 MARCH

✉ Dear Esther

Thank you for agreeing to sponsor my slimming endeavours. I now have you and Jack supporting me. I'll take the sponsor form to church and I think I can get some more sign ups. Do you think I need to open a Support My Cause page online? How much do you think I should try to raise?

You'll never guess who I met at the shops yesterday. I was at Wendleworth's checking out the Easter eggs. Time is short, Easter will soon be with us and once again I was struggling to find Fairtrade eggs. Three aisles of Easter eggs and not a Fairtrade one to be found. Do people not know that there are children enslaved in work on the cocoa plantations?

I was mad. I asked a shop assistant who then had to get his superior to handle my query. Eventually I was seen by a 12-year-old store manager. He asked if it 'really mattered' and reckoned that Fairtrade wasn't quite the same as his favourite brand. I launched into how crazy and uncaring he sounded. He told me to keep my voice down! He is definitely on the hit list to receive emails about the chocolate campaign. Maybe I could sign him up for it?

Oh yes – excuse rant – was saying . . . While in Wendleworth's I saw one of the elders I moaned at from Jacqui's new church. Yes, she has decided to stay there. She's sticking it out and has said: 'it's not so bad' and 'maybe I can make a difference'!

Anyway, I said 'hello' to this elder, but he looked subdued. I think he was with his wife. He seemed henpecked. I went down the baking lane to pick up more food colouring (for all these madly coloured cupcakes) and, I have to admit, had a little giggle to myself at the irony of the situation.

I have been thinking about Suzie recently and I am praying that she finds some church to attend where she can learn and grow. I'm still trying to persuade her to either come to our Hope & Light Church or give your Rivers of Life a punt. Please keep praying for her.

By the way, she did enjoy the open house – phew. I thought it was a great evening. We should do something similar in the summer – perhaps a barbecue. Can't wait for the warmer weather!

So, back to Wendleworth's, I was heading out the door with my towering trolley – do you know a week's shopping these days puts us back over £100; those boys just munch their way through SO much and I guess it'll only get worse as the years go on – when I nearly mowed down Angela. She recognized me as your friend.

She said she had a 'very enjoyable' time at the recent Rivers cheese and wine party and invited me to some do they are having at their house. Geoff didn't say much. Your nickname 'Poor Old Geoff' (POG) is spot on.

It made me so grateful for a husband who is my best friend, not someone just to moan at. Sometimes life is busy and we have shopping list-like conversations so we know what is happening, but that is not what holds us together.

Take care. Speak soon.

Louise

PS I declined Angela's invitation but you might want to prepare yourself for an invitation to a fondue evening . . .

DATE: 16 MARCH

▣ Dear Lou

I can't understand women who do nothing but nag at their spouses. You'd think they'd just be grateful. What a waste of love!

Anyway ... deep thought for today ... So what's your thinking on St Paul and his teaching on 'singleness'. Personally I struggle with it! I think it's on my mind as it would have been my wedding in six months and right now I should be head down preparing for married life.

If you're still looking for fairly traded chocolate eggs then try some of the charity shops. Some sell new products. And you can also go online. Be careful you don't scare the poor Wendleworth's shop manager and his workforce!

I'll pop round and sort out the Support My Cause page for you. They do take a little cut of what you raise but it's a fabulous way of getting people to support your fundraising. Also got choccy eggs for the boys that I need to drop off – fairly traded of course (I got them from a charity shop). Just make sure you hide them so they don't get scoffed ahead of time like last year.

Talking about hungry children. For your slimming cause, why not starving children in Africa? It makes perverted sense. YOU lose pounds by cutting food intake to GAIN pounds for an African food programme? However, for you, it may obviously mean no chocolate!

I may join you in the diet, just for a little while. Have been indulging a little too much myself recently – comfort eating I suppose.

That's a misnomer isn't it? 'Comfort eating!' We eat to make ourselves feel better but it certainly doesn't make us 'comfortable'. The other day I had to lie down on the bed to zip up my favourite jeans ... time to lay off the chocs and cappuccinos for a while, I think!

Esther x

PS I'm not invited to Angela's fondue evening. I wouldn't have accepted it and wouldn't have minded being excluded, except for one thing. She came up to me at choir practice last night to explain that I had probably heard that she and Geoff were having a few people round for fondue on Saturday, and that she didn't want me to be hurt by not being invited but . . . it was an evening for couples only!

I mean, why did she think she needed to explain a non-invitation, that's the question? And why would she think that her explanation would make me feel good about being excluded?

I give up.

DATE: 17 MARCH

✉ Dear Esther

If going round to Angela's house and hitting her with a fondue fork would help, I would. You just don't need this right now.

I realized the six-month wedding date was looming the other day and kept meaning to say I was thinking of you.

And St Paul? I have often wondered if the central message or the key point of his teaching is to be content in whatever situation you find yourself in. For St Paul, married life would have been difficult. He had such a busy life and all those overseas trips. Mind you, Jack is like that. It is really difficult having work and family commitments. Jack does make up for it when he is home though. It's also the cost of his job and it means we have a nice house and can look after the boys and keep up with all their demands. Last week, Ollie asked me yet again for another pair of designer trainers – it's always something. I told him he needed to get a part-time job.

Anyway, back to St Paul . . . Not that I'm comparing my Jack to St Paul, although he is a blessing, but we all have those 'thorns in our side' that can depress us and turn us away from God if we let them. We really want them to push us TOWARDS God.

What was OK for Paul was different for Peter. Peter had a mother-in-law. What was OK for Paul might not be OK for you. What is OK for me might not be OK for you. I know it's not deeply theological, but what do you think?

Louise

PS I wrote to the school-age shop manager yesterday. Awaiting a reply to the egg situation.

✉ Dear Lou

Ahh – mothers-in-law (or is that mother-in-laws?). I miss Harriet. Tom's mum was so lovely and I really miss her. Is that weird? I know she wasn't my mother-in-law, but she nearly was.

Did you know she taught me to knit? My own mum is useless with the needles and Harriet and I really bonded over the wool. I know she was longing for the day when she'd have the opportunity to work a little matinée jacket for her first grandchild. Although I warned her that at my age it might never happen, she lived in hope.

When Tom dumped me (I refuse to say 'broke up' with me) Harriet came round mine and we had a really good cry. You remember? You popped in and caught us sobbing. I can still remember the look on your face when you saw my future mother-in-law in my lounge with a pile of tissues and smeared mascara. By the way, I also still have a memory of those fantastic red velvet chocolate cupcakes you brought over that evening. Although they'll always make me slightly sad, what with the Tom break-up link, they were scrummy!

Mum and Harriet still meet up, I think, to console each other on the fact that they are not soon to be related. I had hoped to stay in touch with my once future-mother-in-law but we're drifting apart. Of course we are. She's Tom's mum and … well … I need to stop here before my brain explodes … but to remain friends with her would just be a bit strange.

Anyway, I asked about the St Paul thing because our Rev Tracey preached on it the other Sunday and I felt I needed to go screaming out of the church I was so mixed up and angry. Don't worry, I resisted the urge. But it got me thinking. Should I be 'grateful' and 'feel blessed' by my singlehood? That's the essence of what Rev T was saying (I think), which is slightly odd because it's usually middle-aged men who come out with those sorts of platitudes. Have you noticed that it's the 'happily married' (aka Angela and the like) or middle-aged men in ministry who say stuff like, 'Blessed are the virgins, for they shall be available for all sorts of good works'? They mean, of course, crèche/ Sunday school/youth clubs/older-people's groups/refreshments . . .

I DO understand that being single means I may not have the distractions that married people have (at least that's the theory) so I guess that, again theoretically speaking, I should be more 'available to God'? But I'm afraid my singleness hasn't yet inspired me to rush off to Asia or deepest Africa on missionary service, nor even to down tools and enter full-time ministry in my own homeland. Surely 'being available' to God is more than that?

However, I'm sure God understands that, no matter one's marital state, there are always 'diversions'. For instance, although I now spend fewer long lonely nights wondering where I went wrong with Tom, all around me I'm surrounded by couples, which is a distraction in itself.

You know, don't you, that the world IS made for couples? The animals went in 'two by two' – isn't that how it goes?

It's getting worse, too. Every time I switch on the TV I seem to be bombarded by 'Christian singles' adverts. 'Are YOU a Christian single looking for a Christian partner? We can help you find God's chosen one! Just pay out X amount every month and we'll get you some dates' – or words to that effect.

I looked up one such dating site on the internet and what I found was very mixed. There were the usual positive messages: 'Thank you so much for this ministry', 'I pray daily for a Chritian partner and now I have hope'. But there were also a load of offensive comments about how these kinds of Christian websites aren't really much better than 'secular' ones. Of course, there were some people who had found them helpful, but the 'anti' camp were very vocal. One correspondent reported that when he/she had repeatedly asked for 'evidence' that ANY person had actually found 'true love' through this particular website the moderator had firmly said, 'This conversation is now closed.'

But it's almost like being brainwashed with the constant drip-drip of these adverts . . . it's a bit like Chinese water torture. I'm now beginning to think, 'Well, why not?'

Surely, despite the lack of evidence of success (at least on that particular internet site) there has to be more than this? On one hand, the Christian in me wants to believe that no Christian business would make false claims or encourage customers to sign up to something that is simply not true. But, on the other hand, the professional in me understands that some people do make all sorts of claims to get business and, so long as they're not breaking any trade description laws, they will push the authenticity of their 'business pitch' to the extreme in order to get orders.

The upshot of all this – don't laugh – is that I did try one site. Actually it was one where you get a couple of 'free searches' so I didn't even have to part with any cash. And I have to say the experience left me feeling rather cynical about the whole process.

During one of my 'free searches' I spotted someone who I thought I recognized. His profile said his name was 'Andrew' and he was 'single' and looking for a 'Christian woman who is aged 25–30, slim build with GSOH'.

However, this chap look remarkably like Garry from your church – you know, the guy who left his family and disappeared? As far as I'm aware he already has a 'Christian woman' – his wife, Janette. She, like him, is around 40, a little on the plump side and I have no idea about her sense of humour but I know she wouldn't find this funny!

The posting was quite old – he entered his details around a year ago – but it was still there. Scary, scary, scary.

E xx

PS Are you planning to come to the Easter Sunday picnic? We could roll our eggs down the hill – the closest you will get to sphereing! ☺

PPS When is Jack's half-marathon?

Dear Esther

I know you miss Harriet but aren't you happy that you're not now going to inherit her two larger-than-life-sized ceramic Pug dogs? If I remember rightly you were a bit spooked when you came back after that first meeting with her and told me that Tom's mum already had you not only married but included in her will – and she would be leaving those precious items to you.

Lucky escape I would say. You are much more a china cat person!

Yes, we will meet you at the 'Churches All Together on the Grand Picnic and Egg Roll Event'. Do you know they are handing out chocolate eggs to people that bring un-churched people to the event? I'm still trying to get the Wendleworth's Fairtrade eggs issue sorted out. I still haven't heard back from Simon the fresh-faced shop manager about the lack of Fairtrade chocolate in his store. I followed up my initial email with a three-page letter, which I dropped in to Wendleworth's the other day, explaining just why the shop should sell fairly traded chocolate – enslaved African children on cocoa plantations and all that.

I can't believe you saw Garry on that website. When I come round next maybe we can check it out and if it is him . . . well, I'm not sure what we can do without becoming interfering busybodies. Or middle-aged detectives.

The half-marathon is next week. Praying for sunny weather! Jack has more than £3,000 in sponsorship. He has done well and everyone has been really supportive. His workmates offered to hire him a fancy dress outfit but he didn't trust them. I had a laugh, thinking about what he could go as.

Louise

DATE: 20 MARCH

🖃 Dear Lou

Thanks for reminding me of the Pugs – I had forgotten that little fact. Anyway, now they'll be destined for some other future daughter-in-law, I guess.

I was quite surprised, as you know, that Harriet embraced me quite so wholeheartedly and so rapidly when I started going out with Tom. It did spook me. I worried that with the age difference between Tom and I, his mother might be a little cautious around this 'older woman' who was stealing her 'little boy'. But far from it. She once told me that she was happy that Tom would have someone to look after him when she was gone. I laughed it off at the time, and joked, 'You'll be around for a long time,' and 'Tom, I think, is a big boy now.' But now, on reflection, I am beginning to think that maybe she had a point. Perhaps Tom WAS just looking for a woman who would look after him. When he came clean with himself and realized that he didn't actually love me and couldn't keep up the charade of an engagement and marriage – well I'm hoping that one day I'll thank him for that but at this moment I . . .

I'm dwelling on this right now because Tom came round the other night to pick up some books he'd left. He's back in the area for the Easter holidays.

It's been more than three months since we broke up and those ridiculous books have been sitting by the front door waiting to be collected. I kept stumbling over them.

I know what you want to know – what did he have to say for himself? Well, nothing much. All he said was, 'How are you? How's work? How's the family?' Nothing of importance, of course. He could barely look me in the eye.

I tried to find out what he wanted to do with the engagement gifts from his family members that at the moment are stored at Mum's. I told him I had sent back those from my side. He said nothing and left.

Enough of that though. Great news on the work front. I have
a couple of new contracts that will keep me busy for a while and
I'll get to travel a little. Nothing exotic, just a couple of paid for
trips to Scotland and deepest Cornwall. It's so hard these days as a
contractor, so any new work is welcome.

Esther

PS I miss that pile of books!

PPS Re Jack's marathon outfit: I think dark suit, bow tie and a martini
(shaken not stirred) but tell him it's best not to carry a firearm.

PPPS Tread carefully with the Fairtrade egg situation. You're beginning
to get a little spooky mad.

✉ Dear Esther

I have endless piles of books – most of which belong to Jack, who
won't get rid of anything. To call him a hoarder is an understatement.
So if you want some rubbish to stack near your front door, just ask.
Happy to gain some floor space.

  I'm sorry these past few days have been difficult for you. At least
now you've seen Tom and you won't have to duck every time you
think you spot him across the road, in the car park or at the cinema.

  What are you bringing to the Easter picnic? Can you manage
hard-boiled eggs without burning them? Don't put them in the
microwave. I invited Simon the store manager. Sent him an email and
delivered an invite. Trying to hold out the olive branch of peace.

Lou

DATE: 22 MARCH

✉ Dear Esther

You will never believe it! Never in my life have I even had a brush with the law – no parking tickets nor even a speeding fine. So what do you think I get through the door this a.m.? An official-looking letter telling me to stop stalking Simon the shop man! At first I couldn't understand what it was about. It took me a while to work out that it referred to my recent conversations and communications with Simon. I am in shock and have a good mind to email him or phone! Too embarrassed to ring and tell you about it. Jack is not happy.

Lou

🗐 Dear Lou

Please, whatever you do, do NOT email, phone or even visit that shop again! Swap allegiance or do an online shop. Or I can get your groceries and stuff.

I'm wearing my official PR hat now. You do NOT want to get into the papers labelled as 'The Mad Fairtrade Woman'. However, if you do find yourself with reporters at the door ring me and I'll come and fend them off for you.

Seriously, I have to say you are being a teeny bit obsessive with this whole chocolate egg thing. Tread carefully, as if on eggshells – this is not eggs-actly normal behaviour. You have written five letters in three days! What is Jack saying?

Esther

DATE: 23 MARCH

✉ Esther

I am overcome with embarrassment. Jack put me right and told me I was being unreasonable. He suggested that it might be hormones and I could have decked him one. Not usually aggressive but that inflamed the situation. Eventually I calmed down and Jack reminded me he loved me. Only wants the best for me.

Can I pretend it was just a yolk? Is it too late to rectify the situation? I still believe in fairly traded chocolate but I admit I was a bit obsessive – maybe got egg on my face? Not eggs-actly my best moment.

Lou – your mad eggcentric friend.

🗒 Dear Lou

Don't worry. We all love you! Maybe you do need a little medical check-up to make sure those old hormones are OK? Just make sure that you talk to Jack whenever you have the urge to write a letter. Emails to old friends are the only exceptions.

Also, tell Jack that they're making a new 007 movie starring the lovely Daniel Craig. It's called *You Only Hoard Things Five Hundred Times*! I heard they're looking for body doubles.

E

PS Did you manage to find a 007 Easter egg, Fairtrade or not?

PPS Talking of hormones, you're not pregnant are you? Although to be fair you are losing weight not gaining it. Just a thought . . .

✉ Dear Esther

No certainly not pregnant. You did get me thinking so I bought a tester kit. Very embarrassing asking for one in the chemist. I found myself wishing at that point I had teenage daughters. I then felt guilty for thinking that too! Anyway, Jack found the packet in the bathroom before I had time to use it.

It was quite funny really. He was holding it in his hand when he called me in to the en suite to say, 'Is there something you need to tell me?'

He was as white as a sheet. Although I knew, in my heart of hearts, that there was no baby, we did have a few moments before the little wand told us otherwise when it did cross my mind that it might be back to nappies and early morning feeds just when we thought we were clear of all that.

But no . . . not expecting. After the tester kit moment, I have to admit I did feel a little sad. Actually, I would not have minded too much.

However, I have booked an appointment with the doctor, just for a check-up. I feel sometimes that I'm losing my mind and am always so stressed out. I also keep forgetting names and words. Maybe it is just my age!

Louise (I think)

DATE: 26 MARCH

🖹 Dear Lou

Don't forget I'm older than you so please don't say 'it's my age'. Makes me feel positively ancient!

MY biological clock is ticking furiously at the moment. I think while I was engaged to Tom I still thought there was a chance of children. Women are having babies later and later, aren't they? I know there was a time when, like you, women mostly had their babies in their 20s. But more and more women now are starting their families later in life – even into their 40s. I know there are risks (I did loads of research on the internet in anticipation) but with marriage finally on the horizon I honestly thought there was a chance for me. Now it seems like it's all over and as a result that old bio clock is bugging me endlessly. There was a christening in church the other week and I'm afraid I had to leave halfway through the service. I came over all emotional. Afterwards, I told Rev Tracey that I had a touch of the hay fever – those wretched lilies in the floral arrangements will do it every time. But I don't think she was convinced.

Oh here's another bit of news on the baby front. My new account manager is pregnant. One of the married ones, as you know, eventually left and I replaced her with a fantastic young woman who, on paper, looked incredibly talented and had loads of potential.

Although you're not allowed to ask in interview if they are planning to have a family anytime soon, and you know if you take on a young woman that it's likely it could happen at some point, it was a bit of a shock when I discovered that she was expecting just a couple of days after she arrived in the office. Leaves me in a bit of a human resources dilemma. She can work for six months or so before maternity leave is due, and she is really very good at what she does. But I'll need another maternity cover part-timer and that's all so costly for us small businesses.

Although I understand the need for women to work, and of course I want to support them – it's important for children to have strong female role models and all that – it's still hard when employees keep popping off to have babies! So pleased to have Colin around. I know you thought it was odd when I appointed a male personal assistant but he is just a lifesaver. Times they are certainly a-changing. And I'm so thrilled they are because, hopefully, Colin won't be taking time off anytime soon to have a baby.

It's so hard not to gripe in public about the pregnancy thing. I have to be so careful around the fertile young women in my office. I don't want them to think my own shrivelling ovaries are making me biased against them. SO pleased I have you to speak my mind to!

E

Life Lines

✉ Dear Esther

Keep smiling! You are amazing and juggle so many things in your life. I'm a fan! I can't say don't worry about the baby thing because that would be just ridiculous. Being a mummy is the best thing that happened to me, I won't deny it. Not a great help, I know.

Changing the subject, I thought this would give you a laugh. I was stuck in some roadworks the other day and was stationary right next to a big advertising hoarding. I was getting really bored – we were there for so long I even turned off my engine to save fuel. Looking around I noticed the advert on the hoarding, displayed large, was actually for one of the Christian internet dating sites. Not sure if it was the same one you looked up, but this was in very poor taste.

In fact, it was so hideous it made me laugh, and I had to take a picture – I'm attaching it.

See what I mean? 'Looking for Love? Want to date a Christian? We are the Love People!'

Oh dear, oh dear, oh dear. What were they thinking? I think the whole 'Love Thy Neighbour' sentiment may have got lost in translation.

On reflection, I think it was much better when we relied on finding our future mates in church, through the usual avenues – Bible classes and 'mixed' evenings involving awkward conversations and/or country dancing where the mere touch of a hand gave a girl the shivers.

I'm just so glad I met Jack at school! Although it means I've never had all the excitement of dating different people, I have avoided all the anguish that some of my friends, like you, have had to endure. I pray for you every day.

God bless.

Lou xx

PS By the way, the roadworks are on Cullan Avenue. Avoid at all costs.

◻ Dear Lou

Thanks for the tip-off. Can't understand why those roadworks are taking so long. It's been months now since they started ploughing up Cullan Avenue and I think the job was only expected to last a couple of weeks. There was a letter in the local paper about it the other day from your Rev. Did you see it? Apparently one of the ladies in your church fell down a hole on the pavement.

Maybe she was heads up looking at the huge dating sign! ☺

Esther

DATE: 27 MARCH

✉ Hi E

Actually it was the Rev's own wife who fell off a very dodgy pavement. We prayed for her in church last Sunday. She wasn't badly hurt, but quite shaken. He was really worried. They are such a devoted couple and he'd be lost without her.

That road has always been a danger. Remember last year it was in such bad disrepair and had so many potholes in it that I ended up with a destroyed tyre? At the time I wondered, rather vocally, where my council tax went. Perhaps they took notice of my complaint and that's why they've drafted in the workforce. So I shouldn't complain that the work is now taking so long.

Lou xx

◻ Hi Lou

I still might have to go down that road though, just to see the appalling ad for myself!

E xx

7

SUBJECT: WHAT A TANGLED WEB WE WEAVE

DATE: 6 APRIL

Dear Louise,

What did the GP say? Are you just 'run down'?

I've managed to get you some more sponsors for your sponsored slim. Rev Tracey thinks it's a great idea and says she'll support you. Watch your Support My Cause page for new entries.

Actually, Rev T is going through a bit of a 'new woman phase'. She's recently bought herself some new outfits and has taken to wearing a little lipstick and mascara, even with her cassock. If I didn't know otherwise, I'd swear she was in love! Now THAT would be radical. And not a little shocking ...

Talking of shocks here's some news.

Now before you take me to task ... I KNOW 'gossip' isn't particularly Christian and you know I'm not in favour – actually never liked it BEFORE I was a Christian so nothing's changed – and we should be, as you've said before, an example to others.   So sharing 'gossip' – information we've heard about others that is absolutely nothing to do with us – is not good in that respect.

All that said, something has come to my attention that I think you would want to be aware of ...

It started with Leggy Lynda at church on Sunday morning. I asked, 'How's it going?' She said, 'Fine ... sort of!' I said, 'Oh sorry,' and she said, 'You know that Jose person who took me home after the Valentine's dance? Well, he's NOT quite what he seems!'

Apparently Jose (who was actually just visiting the area) wasn't looking for a girl after all. Poor old Lynda. He was looking for a man!

Jose, it appears, came to England to look for his sister's boyfriend, who had left her after six months together in Brazil. So he kept asking her questions: Did Lynda know him? Was he a member of her church? Jose has been doing the rounds of the local places of worship hoping to find him. All he knows is that he originally came from this area and attended church here.

Lynda was furious, obviously, and has a rather damaged ego – she definitely thought she'd pulled the gorgeous Jose (who, to rub salt in an already open wound, also turns out to be happily married) and is now spending a good deal of time and effort explaining to anyone who'll listen how her would-be-beau is actually looking for a scumball called Garry, who has impregnated a young Brazilian woman (sister of said Jose) and wasn't that someone who USED to go to 'your friend Louise's church before he deserted his wife and children'?

Lynda, unfortunately, has no qualms about gossip.

I have really agonized over this but I feel someone should take Janette aside and tell her what's been going on with her Garry.

I know we decided NOT to divulge that he'd been masquerading as 'Andrew' on a Christian singles site about a year ago. You were right – it COULD have been his twin brother!

But do you not think that she needs to be made aware of this latest 'news'. It would explain why Garry left the marital home and why he didn't send her any support for upwards of eight months. He wasn't even in the country but living it up and starting a new life (and possibly a new family) in Rio! Looking for his 'inner purpose' eh?

I know this sort of thing happens, but it's just so sad. For everyone. Anyway, I've been praying about whether to tell you but I just wonder whether the news would be better coming from someone in her church rather than Janette finding out via gossip at the school gate.

E x

PS I saw Sam the Boiler Man in the street the other day. We had
quite a nice little chat. It started a little awkwardly with, 'How's your
boiler doing?' but it was all very pleasant.

DATE: 7 APRIL

✉ Dear E

Gosh. It gets messier! Where do you start? All the pieces seem to be
coming together.

Gossip is a difficult thing. Do we gossip too much? We shouldn't
do it – it's as bad a sin as lying or stealing. But we also have to be
wise. What is the next step? When do you leave things alone?

I think when we hear things from a third person we cannot
act on the information straight away. We might just get it
horribly wrong. Best not tell Janette just yet but somehow Garry
needs to be challenged. He is back in the area, I know – Jack told
me he saw him at the gym. I will have a chat to Jack and ask his
advice.

Maybe Jack can talk to Garry.

This sort of mess is such a picture of how our actions become
ripples in a pond.

L

PS Went to doctors and had a blood test. He thinks it may be
hormones. He laughed at the obsessive egg situation.

DATE: 10 APRIL

✉ Dear Esther

I had my blood results back. The kind receptionist gave me a
cancellation. The doctor told me that I am going through an early
menopause. I know Mum went through it early. Runs in families like that.

The doctor remembered me as the Egg Lady but knew eggs-actly what I needed. He suggested a trial of HRT. I know it's officially called 'Hormone Replacement Therapy' but I prefer to convince myself that I'm 'Happily receiving therapy' . . .

L xx

PS Sam, ah what a nice man. OK, I'll be quiet now!

✉ Dear Lou

Glad you are receiving therapy. The question is – is it making you happy?

Good idea about the Garry situation. Let Jack handle it. After all, what's the point of being James Bond if you can't sort out a tricky situation?

Now I can stop worrying.

Esther

DATE: 11 APRIL

✉ Hi Louise

Just thought you'd like to know that I went past Wendleworth's this morning and guess what? There's a fantastic poster in the window announcing the arrival of Fairtrade Easter eggs! I went in – they don't know you're my friend so I managed to sneak through security – and I saw a magnificent display of said eggs.

AMAZING! Simon has seen the light – now that's prophetic. A 12-year-old was tweaking the display and I approached him and saw his 'Simon: Manager Pleased to Help You' badge and congratulated him on the introduction of Fairtrade. I asked him where he had the idea and he said, 'We've introduced the eggs due to customer concern and encouragement.'

I think I responded with something like, 'Well, thank goodness you got them JUST in time for Easter – a few days more and you'd have missed it!'

So there you are. Your 'concern and encouragement', despite the threat of imprisonment, has made a difference! Sometimes taking a stand can be costly but definitely worth it.

You can now call off OO7's planned assault on the store to smuggle Fairtrade eggs in overnight (tell Jack I still think that's such a great idea).

Esther xx

✉ Hi Esther

Not sure OO7 would have been up for it anyway. He's still recovering from the half-marathon. Even though it was a couple of weeks back, he's still suffering.

When he decided against the fancy dress, I told him to wrap up warm but he would insist on going out on that freezing morning in just his skimpy shorts and vest. You saw him when he crossed the line – he was blue and that wasn't just the shorts! I was SO glad for our winter woollies that day and I have to say, that magnificent ski jacket looked AMAZINGLY warm! Colourful but very snug.

Jack still hasn't shaken off the man flu and not even the sight of the half-marathon medallion, which is still displayed proudly on the mantelpiece, perks him up.

L

DATE: 13 APRIL

✉ Dear Esther

How do you fancy a lasagne – or three?

No, I haven't gone mad and started a lasagne business. I currently have eight full-sized lasagnes on my kitchen surfaces. They are absolutely everywhere.

Now, you do know that lasagne is Jack's favourite dish? Of course! You do – and so, it seems, does everyone else in town.

As explained, Jack is still under the weather and last Sunday we didn't make it to church – the boys were out late on Saturday and Jack and I decided to have a lie-in. Apparently in the morning service there were special prayers for 'the sick of the church' and our Rev said, 'Let's pray for Jack, Louise and the family. Jack is far from well and Louise is having to cope with everything on her own.' Not exactly how I would have put it as I do tend to do most of the household chores and duties even when Jack is not laid low. But anyway, within hours stuff started being left on our doorstep.

There were a couple of cakes – interesting given I'm a cake maker but very kind. There was a bottle of whisky and a hamper of fruit and half a dozen lasagnes, all ready to go in the oven. A couple went in the freezer and we enjoyed the others over the next few days.

But while the cakes, booze and fruit have dried up, the lasagne keeps coming. I hardly dare open the front door most mornings. I am now drowning in the stuff and the boys, and even Jack, have absolutely refused point blank to take another mouthful of pasta.

It is very kind of our friends, but unless someone takes some of the dishes off my hands, I fear I might have to throw them out. After all the fundraising for the starving African children that goes against my conscience.

So would you like some – for eating now and for your freezer? Please feel free to come round and take away several. Maybe the account managers and Colin would like one each too? Sam has already taken away a couple and I also got Jack to drop one round to James – it's definitely all over between him and Catherine and he's moved out. Jack and Sam helped him move his stuff and when Jack came home he was quite emotional about it all. He says James is at a loss – he can't understand why what he thought was the perfect marriage just crumbled. He's finding life really hard, and he's finding church perhaps the hardest part – difficult questions and all that. Catherine hasn't really made much of an appearance recently but James has been trying, although has taken to sneaking in during the first hymn to hide

Life Lines

behind a pillar and then leaving before the benediction to avoid the rush of sympathy and awkward glances over lukewarm tea/coffee.

Anyway, any ideas for ending the flow of lasagnes gratefully received.

Lou xxx

✉ Dear Louise

Many thanks for the offer of the lasagnes. They'll go down a treat. Colin is a veggie but the account managers and their families will be very grateful. I'll pop round after house group.

Only thing I can suggest to stem the tide of pasta is an appearance at church on Sunday morning.

E xx

PS I bumped into Catherine in Wendleworth's the other day – we literally bumped into each other when I rounded the corner of the cereals/toilet roll aisle. I drew a breath and put on my 'sad this has happened to you' face and cautiously asked, 'How's it all going Catherine?' She seemed remarkably chipper. 'Oh fine. James has moved out, which isn't great for the girls but he's not far away, so they're OK about it, I think,' was her reply.

She certainly didn't seem to be in mourning. Sorry to hear James is suffering. I'm still reeling a bit from it as well. They DID appear to be a perfect couple. But as I've said before – you never can tell . . .

8

SUBJECT: A TIGHT SPOT

DATE: 28 APRIL

✉ Hiya Esther

What a lovely Easter we had! After that freak blizzard the week before, I really wondered if we'd make it out the door. Why are we English SO unable to cope with the white stuff?

It was great to see you on Easter Saturday. Wasn't it amazing that the snow seemed to miraculously thaw overnight, just in time? I have to say the sight of your Rev Tracey and St Peter's Father Sean rolling eggs down that hill will live with me for quite a while. Cassocks hitched up round their knees and dog collars thrown to the wind! Hilarious. They seem to get on very well which, Jack happened to mention, is doing great things for ecumenical relations.

At last Jack was himself again. What a godsend! No more coughing and spluttering and sneezing. I know I joked about the man flu but he really did feel grim for a while. We are now down to one lasagne a week – what did we do in the days before freezers?

So glad we got to sit together at the Joint Churches Vigil on Saturday night. Have to say it was very snug in the pew. Couldn't believe that the heating failed. I do hope it wasn't TOO cosy for you and Sam. LOL!

When we got home the boys were determined to open their Easter eggs and make a start on them – it was quarter past midnight so 'officially Easter Sunday' and Jack and I didn't have the energy to argue.

And yes, the boys are now allowed on the sofa. It's all mended!

But as we opened our Fairtrade eggs (Jack went in to Wendleworth's to buy them. Although I'm not under any court injunction I took your advice and stayed clear of the place) I was reminded that this is SUCH an important moment in our Christian life. We had amazing services on Good Friday and Easter Sunday morning. I can't believe I let the matter of some chocolate eggs divert me from the real meaning of Easter. I guess that's what happens when you take your eye off the ball, or even the egg.

I've been reading my Bible a lot more recently, which has been much needed. Thanks for the information about that website with all the women-centred Bible notes and prayer articles. I'm glad it's also helping you! Are you serious about us attending that Proverbs 31 women's group? Are we getting holy in our old age?

How did Penny's wedding go on Easter Monday? Love to hear all the news. Saw the picture of you on Facebook in your outfit. Must say you looked fabulous – that shopping trip was worthwhile. ☺

Update on the Garry saga. Since he returned home from his trip away to 'find his inner purpose' he has stayed away from church and has been living with a relative I believe. But over Easter he turned up. What was worse was that he was sitting next to me for communion.

I wasn't sure what to do as Janette was across the aisle giving him the daggers – she has not heard from him for months! In the end the church agreed to help them financially as they had not had a bean from him. They have two little girls and I felt so sad for them sitting there in church, giving their daddy a little wave and he trying not to look across so as not to upset his estranged wife even more.

But what to do with the communion? As the bread and wine started to circulate the building I was in a dilemma. Eventually I decided. I held the bread and said, 'Garry this is for you. Jesus has forgiven you but you need to act in repentance.'

He said, 'What for? What have I done wrong?' At this point, in the middle of 'Thine be the Glory' I passed the bread and wine to Sam, who was sitting the other side of Garry. What I really wanted to do was to thump the man and tell him to wise up – in Christian love, of course!

Sam smiled and nodded as if to say I had done the right thing. After the last hymn our Reverend hurried across and extracted Garry to his office before there was uproar.

Isn't our church family made up of all sorts? You couldn't make up half of what goes on. And we are meant to be examples and ambassadors. Aren't we? God give us grace.

Sam was sweet. He came over at the end of the service and told me I was very brave saying something to Garry. Apparently the man's antics in Brazil are common knowledge. I feel so sad for Janette and the little ones. But I also feel I did the right thing. I know people have to settle their relationship with God for themselves, and seek forgiveness where it is necessary, but we should also challenge our brothers and sisters if we know they are doing something wrong, shouldn't we?

I don't know if you will see Garry but I know they live in your street so he may turn up. I thought it was worth warning you that he's definitely back in the area. I am all for restoration but there seems to be many steps that need to happen first.

Signing off . . .

Louise
(Who is happy as she lost 4lb this week. That small Eastern European country I recently resembled has lost a stake of its border and Africa is gaining pounds as the sponsors stack up!)

✉ Dear Lou

Thanks for the warning. Yes, Janette still lives nearby. She's nice but you know, until you told me that Garry was an elder in your church when he disappeared last year, I had no idea they were Christians . . . well I suppose it's not written on people's foreheads!

If I recall, this is the man who about three years ago made an official complaint to the council about my neighbour Mrs Francis. You know her — she's the one with the purple rinse who makes me the lovely casseroles because I occasionally do her shopping for her.

Her drains were all blocked up and just a little bit smelly but rather than offering to help unblock them, Garry popped a really nasty note through her door and then promptly called the council. She was really upset. I'm SO glad I didn't know he was a 'Christian'. I wouldn't have been able to defend such unneighbourly behaviour. Everyone in the street was just glad when he went off the scene. Isn't that terrible? Even Janette looks happier, truth be told.

Glad to hear you're shrinking. I say that in the nicest possible way!

Esther

PS Would you like me to get you some publicity for your sponsored slim? I could get a little article in the paper if you want? They could take pics? I've even thought of a title for your endeavours . . . 'Pounds for Africa'!

✉ Hi Esther

Great title but please let me think about it, as I'm not sure I want everyone in the neighbourhood knowing how much I weighed/weigh. And I am not that photogenic! Can't see why anyone would want photos of me ☺ But it would be excellent publicity! So, let me chew it over some more. Got to feel comfortable with it all.

By the way, Sam is also looking for some help with publicity and I told him to get in touch. Hope you don't mind!

Lou

DATE: 29 APRIL

🖹 Hi Lou

Will patiently await any decisions you make re publicity. But don't put yourself down, Sam the Boiler Man has already been in touch and we're meeting to discuss things next Monday. And before you jump to any conclusions . . . IT'S NOT A DATE! We're meeting in The Crooked Teapot and are going to look at sample leaflets with a view to me possibly helping him with his new business cards and publicity materials.

If you can wangle romance into that then you're a better woman than I am.

E

9

SUBJECT: AIRING IT IN PUBLIC

Dear Lou

My washing machine is on the blink again. I know you said I could come round anytime to do my laundry at yours but, knowing how much muddy sporting gear you have to cope with as the football season draws to a close, I decided to pay a little visit to the launderette. Your machine must be on the go 24/7.

So, two things happened – why do they always happen to me?! There I was in the launderette working on my laptop (I had an urgent report to complete) and occasionally raising my head to watch the world and my smalls spin around, when the oddest chap walked in.

I instantly guessed he was a Christian. He was carrying a huge striped bag of washing with 'Cleanliness is next to godliness' emblazoned on it. But what really gave away his identity were the white sports socks teamed with Jesus sandals, and the T-shirt bearing the logo for the 'Friends for Jesus' summer event . . . you know, the one where masses of Christians descend on a field in the middle of nowhere for ministry, mud, music, men-spotting and madness.

I tried to ignore him but it was pretty hard.

He started telling the elderly lady in the corner all about Friends for Jesus and how he was looking forward to it. Then he began relating details of the sermon he had enjoyed in church the previous Sunday, which was all about celibacy and purity. The poor woman couldn't escape.

The radio was on in the corner of the room and just at that point a song came on that mentions 'going to bed' . . .

Well, that was when it all kicked off.

Jesus Sandals Man turned nasty, called the launderette manager from the office at the back and pronounced that the song was 'disgusting', that he was a Christian and they should turn it off. It was 'of the devil' and, by allowing this song to play out on the radio in a public place, the launderette was encouraging promiscuity, under-age sex and unwanted pregnancies.

By the time he'd completed his rant, of course, the song was over. I was SO embarrassed. Maybe I should have said something but by this time the man was red in the face and looked like he was going to explode. I thought if I stood up and said, 'Well, I'M also a Christian and it's only a song,' I might have been forced into a theological argument, in public, with an unreasonable bigot. I didn't have the stomach for it and also felt it would be rather destructive. The sight of two Christians having an incomprehensible theological ding-dong about something quite so trivial would not, I believe, have been a good advert for Christianity.

So I endured the man's rant during the final spin of my washing, packed up my washing in double time and rushed back to my car.

When I got home, after a detour to the supermarket and having consumed two chocolate bars, I started putting away my washing. Unfortunately I noticed several pairs of men's Y-fronts and a couple of extra T-shirts. I had a feeling I knew to whom they belonged and I did feel like putting them in bin. But they were quite new so I didn't. I bundled them into a bag and headed back to the launderette.

Trying to explain to the manager just how I'd managed to acquire the Jesus Sandals Man's private particulars was hard, because I had absolutely no idea how they'd got into my 'clean wash' basket. But as I handed over the T-shirts and Y-fronts to the manager I was overwhelmed with a sense that I needed to apologize for the rude Christian man to whom I guessed they belonged.

It was then that I was struck by what I was actually doing. Here I was, a fairly attractive single women clutching a pair of men's tidy whities, insisting to an uninterested launderette manager that not all Christians were mad about sex or basically bonkers!

I am now home with clean knickers and a somewhat tarnished reputation.

But, as I've sat here having a strong coffee, I've got to thinking. WHY did those Y-fronts get into my wash? Was it because I'd have to return to the shop to hand them over and that would give me an opportunity to prove to the manager that not all Christians are crazy?

I've heard the expression 'God works in mysterious ways' but never would I have guessed that he would work through men's underpants!

Esther

✉ Dear Esther

Gosh, you need Sam in to help you sort things out. Not to prevent you getting your knickers in a twist – I meant to sort out your machine!

However, I do think you were right to explain that that mad Christian was wrong. We have to be very sensitive in how we speak and react. What are we called to be? 'IN the world but not OF it'? But that often means the world does not understand us. We are an unusual bunch of people. Some of us more unusual that others.

How did the laundry man react to it all?

Lou x

PS If you are developing a men's pants fetish happy to supply some in all shapes and sizes!

DATE: 14 MAY

✉ Dear Lou

Actually the guy at the launderette was really nice about it. He said
Jesus Sandals Man is a regular in the place and always has something
to moan about, is always spouting the Bible and trying to ram it
down other people's throats. I felt so embarrassed for the Christian
faith. It really was a case of 'What would Jesus do?'

The guy said it was the first time anyone else had come in
and apologized for unreasonable Christian behaviour and he
appreciated it. Not sure that my little weird 'witness' involving the
Y-fronts will endear him to the faith though, if Jesus Sandals keeps up
his 'evangelizing'.

Esther

DATE: 15 MAY

✉ Hi E

I've often wondered why as Christians we are known more for what
we stand AGAINST rather than what we stand FOR.

We can make such a fuss about things and sometimes we have to
ask ourselves – do these trivial things we obsess about really matter
when there are so many more important issues that we might be
fighting for, such as world hunger, people who are victims of human
trafficking and the lack of decent health care for the vast majority of
children in the world? (You guessed it, I've been watching another TV
documentary!) And we also have to be careful not to insist that people
live the same way as we do. We need to choose our battles carefully
and all that.

However, you remember I did go into a newsagent when the kids
were small and asked them to cover their lads' mags? They were very
helpful and did just that. That was definitely a 'small battle' worth

fighting. It's proved, to me at least, that not everyone is against us if we can formulate a good reason for our requests. Must remember that when another Fairtrade Easter egg moment takes me over!

Louise

DATE: 20 MAY

🖃 Dear Lou

Washing machine fixed. No more trips to the launderette required. When Sam and I met for coffee to talk about his marketing plans, I mentioned the failing machine and he came round that night. He IS chivalrous. He wouldn't even take money for the work, so I repaid him for his kindness by inviting him to share supper. Don't worry, I didn't cook. We had a takeaway.

He was in stitches when I told him the saga of the launderette. He did suggest we go evangelizing around all the launderettes in the region – telling them that Jesus can make them clean. I hurled a cushion at him.

Esther

✉ Esther

It sounds like your heart is in a spin!

🖃 Lou

No heart or head spinning Louise, but we DID have a great evening!

E

10

SUBJECT: BIRTHDAY TREATS

DATE: 30 MAY

Dear Louise

Greetings from sunny Glasgow – NOT!

It's been lashing it down ever since I got north of Manchester! I decided to drive to this conference because I thought I'd enjoy the scenery en route, but all I got to see through the windscreen wipers was the occasional glimpse of a mist-shrouded hill and the tail lights of the vehicles in front.

Never mind, because the conference has been excellent and I'm staying in a great hotel. It even has a spa – not jealous are you? ☺

My presentation went well. I was doing two sessions for people who wanted/needed to learn more about 'Doing big PR . . . with a twist' (basically doing PR on a tight budget – my speciality).

People had to sign up in advance for their chosen seminars and my first session, before lunch on the second day, was attended by about a dozen people. I was very happy, even though I'd been put in what could only be described as a breezy conservatory, which also served as a through route from the main auditorium to the toilets.

Session two was after lunch and I had a similar number of people signed up to attend. So imagine my shock when the conservatory started to fill up. At first I thought that maybe delegates were suffering the aftershock of a rather dodgy prawn cocktail (I steered clear) and just needed to be near to the bathrooms, but then it was obvious that, actually, they were there for MY seminar!

That session was attended by around seventy-five people. People were standing in the doorways! I had to change everything I was planning to do – first time round people got together to discuss issues in little groups but this time I had to assign team leaders to ensure things didn't get out of hand. It was wonderful! I thoroughly enjoyed it and was buzzing.

However, I was somewhat confused. WHY had so many people turned up to my little session? Presumably it meant that they hadn't attended the other seminars available in that slot – 'How to work with a £1m budget', 'Celebrity booking' and 'Making the most of your TV ad campaigns'. And yes, I heard later that those sessions were pretty poorly attended after lunch.

Over pre-dinner drinks I got my answer. One woman who had attended my session came up and shook my hand and told me how much she had enjoyed it. She represents a small charity and said she'd felt rather depressed by day two because all the main presentations were from experts who had multi-million pound budgets. That is completely out of her understanding and, therefore, the solutions they were offering were completely out of her range of possibilities.

Over lunch she'd reported as much to another delegate who'd said, 'Oh you need to go to the seminar in the room next to the toilets. There's a woman there who gave us some tips on how to do PR on a shoestring.' Apparently the word got round – hence the large numbers.

I've always known that my chosen 'industry' will often give the impression that unless you pay big bucks and get celebrities on board, you'll fail at PR. If you remember, that's exactly why I set up my agency, to help the 'small people' who have limited budgets. What I didn't realize was that there are quite SO many people out there trying to do PR with no money whatsoever.

So, all in all, a very, very good day for me.

You know that I've often thought I should consider changing my career to something more 'useful' (Christian-wise) but after today I really feel I'm contributing to the world.

I'm leaving Glasgow at lunchtime tomorrow and have decided to drop off in the Lake District after all, to see Penny and Clive. She's been pestering me to visit ever since the wedding and if she finds out from Facebook that I've been north of Watford she'll be upset that I didn't make the effort.

Hope all is well with you all.

I know I said it before I left but – Happy Birthday!

Sorry I wasn't there – only another year to the big 40. ☺

And how did Bobby's birthday go? Did you manage to cope with a houseful of teenagers?

Love

Esther

DATE: 31 MAY

✉ Dear E

So pleased I am in the warmer south. Cold and I do not go together. I've decided that my favourite holiday destinations have to be above 20 °C. I'd be no good in the Canadian north or on the ski slopes!

The conference sounds great – really fantastic! So pleased that the seminars went well. I have to say when you tried your presentation on me before you departed it went completely over my head. But it was very impressive!

BTW the other day a lovely leaflet dropped through my letter box announcing the new and improved 'Jackson Boiler and Plumbing Services'. Ingenious of you to put Sam's own smiling face on the front with his personal greeting, 'Hi, I'm Sam and I'm Jackson Boiler and Plumbing Services.' SO friendly. If Sam wasn't my plumber already I think I'd have to ring him up and invite him for a plumbing consultation. Just don't tell Jack! I know Sam was a little worried about making the leaflet quite so personal and that he'd have preferred something a bit more 'technical' (what is it about men and pictures of engines, or in Sam's case, U-bends and toilets?) but I think it's done the trick. I am sure he will have lots of elderly ladies ringing up for his services. He has such a kind face.

Now to the party.

Please, please, please when Laurence reaches 15 remind me NOT to agree to a weekend house party.

When Ollie had his (can you believe he's going to be 17 in a few weeks?) it was fine. Perhaps it's because Oliver is a different character and has only a few close friends, all of them quite quiet really. Bobby is a different kettle of fish, as they say.

Having Bobby's birthday the day after mine – I'll always remember THAT birthday, spent pushing and shoving for England – means once again my own special day was spent preparing for his. Don't mind so much, in fact it's a bit of a birthday tradition – me making birthday cake and parties for other people's children as well as my own.

This time round we were expecting six overnight 'guests' and, instead, got twelve.

There were teenage boys everywhere. We had two tents in the garden housing two boys apiece – Jack is STILL moaning about the damage done to the turf, especially as we've not had a drop of rain here for weeks and his precious green lawn is beginning to resemble the Gobi Desert!

There were three boys in Bobby's room, not including him, three in the lounge and two in Laurence's room – he was on a blow-up bed in Ollie's attic, which pleased said older brother no end!

They all arrived on Friday night. We thought that they would want to go out for the evening but they'd decided on a games night and pizza. They ploughed their way through four extra-large pepperoni paradise pizzas, three margheritas, two Hawaiians and one giant-sized 'Alfonso' – this is apparently a speciality of the pizza shop in town and consists of a mixture of slices with toppings that look like the contents of a slops bucket! I love pizza – one of

my weaknesses and very bad for any slimming plan – but even I
could not stomach a slice of that!

The boys and their guests also managed to consume several tubs of
ice cream, gallons of fizzy drinks and the entire contents of the biscuit
barrel. But at least, as Jack consoled me as we crawled into bed while
the party still proceeded downstairs, we had to be happy that they
were not out drinking!

Saturday dawned late for most. It's at times like this I am SO
grateful for an en suite in the master bedroom, although both Ollie
and Laurence did sneak in to use our shower!

Jack was out running, as per usual on Saturday morning. So it
was down to me to 'do' brunch, during which the boys cleared us
out of every scrap of cereal in the house, ate four loaves of toast and
finished off every smidgen of jam within a four-mile radius. I did
think about making American pancakes but decided I was too tired,
so I offered them chocolate croissants.

I know you're going to think us mad but Jack and I escaped early
Saturday evening. The boys were all going to the park to play football
and promised not to make a mess on their return, so we went to the
cinema. Haven't been for ages and it was going to be a wonderful
night – a real birthday treat. Unfortunately we both fell asleep within
ten minutes of the lights descending and only woke up when a man
poked us awake at the end of the film by saying, 'You can stop snoring
now! It's all over!'

We got home around 11 p.m. to find . . . yes, you've guessed it
. . . the whole house overrun with teenagers – both boys and girls. We
heard them before we opened the door. Apparently the word had got
around that there was a party at ours and the whole of the south of
England had decided to descend.

I'm surprised you didn't hear the music from your hotel in
Glasgow! There were kids everywhere. Some had got into Jack's
precious collection of wines. (Thankfully they had not found the
spirits). We do not drink a lot so have had some of the bottles for
years but it's all gone now. Of course, what goes in has to come out
so a number of them had subsequently had to visit the bathrooms. My

en suite will never again feel like the pleasant haven away from the
world that it once was.

Worse still, some of the kids had found my larder and had brought
out the Pentecost cupcakes that were all ready for the Pentecost
picnic on Bank Holiday Monday. And I had been so proud of the
decoration on those cakes! To add insult to injury, they also consumed
my birthday cake.

The whole house was in uproar. Jack and I returned to find Oliver
screaming at his brother's 'friends', 'MY MUM IS GOING TO KILL
YOU!', a traumatized Laurence barricaded in the downstairs toilet
and Bobby sitting quietly in a corner trying not to cry.

Our arrival saved the day. We managed to clear the house of
strangers without calling the police, but Jack was insistent that the
home be put back into some sort of order immediately, so Bobby, Ollie
and the twelve 'weekend friends' were up until the early hours washing
floors, sweeping up broken plates and generally trying to make amends.

I, on the other hand, realizing that the mob had munched their
way through the entire Pentecost picnic cupcake order sat crying in
my larder for about fifteen minutes while Jack eventually managed
to extract Laurence from the toilet. All Jack could say was, 'At least
there were no drugs,' and 'If this is the worst that they do . . .' He was
so solid, a real hero – my OO7.

Sunday dawned quiet. The 12 disciples disappeared quickly. None
of them dared ask for breakfast – by 7.30 a.m. I was in the kitchen
frantically baking and there was a dark cloud over the whole general
area. I am afraid I was not a loving or kind mum! Grace had left the
kitchen.

And even church was out, which was a real shame since it was
Pentecost!

Bobby swore it wasn't his fault but is now 'grounded' for the
rest of eternity. Oliver should have known better and despite his
protestations of, 'There was nothing I could do!' is not in our best
books.

As for Laurence, well we've discovered why he was traumatized.
Apparently just before we arrived back home he'd gone up to the

attic to try to go to sleep on his blow-up bed, only to find a couple of young people making out. We are not sure what exactly went on as he did not want to talk about it.

We have always been clear with the boys that sex is a gift from God, something for marriage and not before. But I think this is something we need to talk about further. I'm beginning to realize that we may have skirted around the meatier issues such as under-age sex, unwanted pregnancies and sexually transmitted diseases. Of course, we are aware that the kids know all about the birds and bees and we did the simple stuff (actually it was left to me) but I guess, like many parents, we have left the 'main education' to school. It also makes me wonder how much teaching is done in church. I do fear that it's rather limited because of the natural reticence of us Christians to talk about sex.

I've become aware over the years that we have to be careful that the boys don't have their views of intimate matters shaped entirely by 'the world'! Some of the issues are as simple as 'How far do you go?' When I was a teenager kissing for more than three seconds was not allowed and French kissing was unheard of. I want our boys to have real relationships where they commit to their girlfriends, know when to stop and feel that sex should be protected for marriage. I know we can't force our way upon them, but it is an ideal that I still hold out for.

So – we've that to come. Soon Jack and I will need to have a more serious talk with our children and lay it all on the line. The older boys know it and are dreading it but there needs to be a real openness about this conversation, when it happens. Laurence is aware that something GIGANTIC is on the family agenda but isn't aware of the enormity of what is about to land. Meanwhile, the blow-up bed has gone to the dump!

This has all been a real parenting challenge with lots of ups and downs, disappointment and despair, yet moments of pride as we saw the boys trying to gain control of the situation, and knuckling down to make amends. It was hard not to blow a fuse completely but Jack and I also understood that the situation was not irredeemable.

I SO wish you'd been around just to cry with me (and laugh – I know that's what would have happened) and help with the second batch of Pentecost cupcakes! But they turned out great anyway, even if I didn't think the decoration was perfect. I was still frosting and sprinkling with little silver balls and other stuff at 2.30 a.m. on Bank Holiday Monday morning. We attended the Pentecost picnic but I fell asleep under a tree and missed most of it!

Sam was amazing. We had to call him out on Sunday morning before church to unblock the main toilet. Of course, we had to explain what had occurred. Jack and I were dreading what he might find – given the previous evening's activities of a bedroom nature it could have been absolutely anything – but it turned out to be nothing more sinister than a hand towel. Why someone felt the need to rifle through my airing cupboard, find a fancy hand towel and try to flush it down the pan is anyone's guess.

No loss though. They were given to me by my sister Darcy and I never really liked them. Too much lace!

So, what started out as an innocent party weekend, which we thought would be cheaper than hiring a hall to help Bobby welcome in his 16th year, turned out to have much more than a financial cost.

Give my love to Penny and Clive and see you when you get back.

Love

Louise

PS If you can bottle some of that Glasgow rain, Jack and the garden will be eternally grateful.

PPS And, of course, I completely forgot to say thanks for my pressie!

DATE: 1 JUNE

⌨ Dear Lou

Oh dear. Keep smiling!

Thought the gift would make you smile. You did say a while back that you want to try sphereing and the voucher allows you to take a friend – I thought Jack might like it? He's the active one of the two of you, after all. The little stuffed hamster was just to make you smile.

E xx

PS What era did you grow up in? French kissing was all the rage in my day. Or maybe it's just because I'm half French Canadian! xx

✉ Dear Esther

Have to say the sphereing voucher was a bit of a shock. But a good one.

Jack and the boys howled with laughter. But when he realized it was voucher for two, Jack did pale a little. I think he might be all mouth and no action on this one!

I'll show those boys! I'm thrilled – if a little scared.

Glad I'm losing a bit of weight though; in my previous state I risked hurtling faster in that hamster ball than probably would be safe.

Lou xx

DATE: 2 JUNE

⌨ Dear Louise

Greetings from the Lakes!

Penny's landed on her feet. Always presumed that Clive was minted but I think he actually might be a co-owner of the Mint.

They live in a beautiful five-bedroomed home overlooking Lake Windermere! They even have their own jetty for their own speed-boat. You'd think with all that water they wouldn't need a pool, but they have one anyway. Heated indoor, with an opening roof and an accompanying hot tub. Who needs spa hotels? So glad I have a new cozzie with matching wrap.

My minor jealousies aside, I'm very happy for the newly minted Penelope. Even though she's struggling a little with the three grown-up step-children who are not over happy about their new 'Mama', she manages to stay calm most of the time.

They send their love!

Glad you liked the Jackson Boiler and Plumbing Services leaflet. It reminds me I didn't tell you that just before I headed north I had an awkward conversation with someone at church who also wanted me to do some PR for them – he owns a little company that is also struggling in the economy. After I spoke to him I emailed a formal quote for the work and I got a really snotty email back saying he was a 'Christian brother' and he hadn't expected to be charged.

What he didn't realize was that I know that last year he paid over the odds for PR from one of my local competitors. I wrote back and told him that, unfortunately, I haven't yet managed to win the lottery or perform the miracle of the loaves and fishes – I still have to eat! I was a bit more polite than that – I AM in PR after all – but that was the gist.

He hasn't replied and obviously, being away from home, I haven't seen him yet. I guess I won't be on his Christmas card list this year!

Just WHY is it that in the Christian world there's this expectation that everyone will/wants/is able to do everything 'for nothing' – especially when it involves using our professional skills? There are times I'm willing to do stuff for free but this is my paid job. Don't we read somewhere in the Bible, 'A workman is worth his hire'?

Just to put you at ease, Sam insisted on paying for the PR. I did give him a good deal, of course! There are always perks in running one's own business, you can decide to whom you give the discounts. And I know I've received enough reciprocal benefits in the shape of washing machine and boiler maintenance!

I popped into that little shop in Kendal you told me about and picked up your supply of mint cake. They don't do the diet variety. I tried a morsel and the sugar rush had me awake for hours.

See you when I get back.

Esther

✉ Dear Esther

Thank you for being so supportive. Africa also thanks you. I have lost another couple of pounds and my Support My Cause tally has gone up another couple of hundred. Great but craving cake!! Maybe it's those hormones . . .

And I think it was right of you to expect payment for that PR work. But it is awkward, isn't it? It is best being clear right at the start. You don't want any difficult situations. Mind you something like that happened to us once. We were going on holiday and I had some nice paper I wanted to use to decorate the living room. I mentioned it to someone at church, saying that I would love to surprise Jack by having the living room decorated for when we returned home.

This lady told me she knew someone who could do it and I was NOT to pay her as it was a gift, her treat. She was very insistent because Jack had helped her with something in the past. So kind of her. We went on holiday and yes, Jack was surprised by the redecorated lounge. I was even more surprised to find a bill for £200. The 'kind lady' had changed her mind when the bill came in. It was so awkward. We had to borrow the money to pay the bill.

Then there have been other times when God has really blessed us by the kindness of others who have done things we really did not expect. It's at those times that we are bowled over by people's generosity – and it's surprising how often those little gifts have come just at the time when we were short of funds, or struggling.

God knows what we need, and he is willing to bless us. We've proved that so many times over the years.

Lou

☐ Dear Lou

Was that the nice posh paper with the silver fleck? That was really badly put up. I don't think you should have paid the bill! Didn't you have to replace it within the year?

E x

✉ E

Yes. Harsh – don't remind me! It really wasn't a treat and turned out to be a cowboy job, a nightmare!

L x

11

SUBJECT: SUMMER MADNESS

DATE: 7 JULY

✉ Dear Esther

Can you stand this weather? I can't. So hot and bothered. Not sleeping well. Jack thinks I am also having night sweats.

I've always secretly thought I should have been a missionary but I'm thinking I might have had to opt for good works somewhere north of the tundra, rather than the obvious tropics.

And the boys are driving me mad! They are so grumpy and snippy – I know it's the heat. I'll be SO happy when they disappear to football camp at the end of term. That sounds awful, but if I have to act as referee for yet another silly argument I'll scream.

The start of the summer holidays is always a bit of a trial but this year I give particular thanks to God for church-run camps! They are a blessing to any harassed parent and maybe the boys (party lovers included) will learn a little more about our loving and forgiving Father.

As you know, the past weeks have been pretty grim for us post party apocalypse! I'm so grateful to have you as a friend. When you rang up the other afternoon and said, 'Want to come out to play?' I could have screamed with delight.

OK, so it was only a walk and an ice cream but it was bliss! By the way, you forgot to tell me where you got that enormous floppy hat. Loved it. Wish I'd had one as my neck got quite sunburnt!

Back to camp. Oliver is threatening not to go, because he's worried that Chloe will ditch him and go off with Lewis – you know, the arch enemy.

Since Jack and I had THE BIG CONVERSATION with the boys
Oliver has been a bit quiet. First we thought it was just because he
was mortified to hear his parents speak about sex in such frank terms.
I bet you he'd kidded himself that his mum and dad only ever had sex
three times, just to create him and his brothers, so to hear us talk so
candidly must have been a bit of a shock.

Like most teens, he has girls on the brain, and is convinced that if
he goes off to football camp the dastardly Lewis will try to capture
Chloe's heart. Jack and I sat him down and explained that we'd
already paid for the week's camp and if he wanted to cancel he'd
have to pay us for it. When he realized that it meant no pocket money
until he was 45, he decided that maybe Chloe could be trusted.

So much for brotherly love – Bobby has a bet with his friend that
Chloe will go off with Lewis as soon as the church minibus pulls out
of the car park with football campers on board. Ollie found out and is
mad, mad, mad!

Laurence, as usual, is still deciding which side to take. He
understands all the relationship stuff a little bit more now, but still
thinks the idea of anyone having sex is simply disgusting. We were
watching something on TV the other night and he left the room when
a couple started kissing on screen. When Jack went to find him he was
sitting in the kitchen having a lemonade waiting for the 'blow-up bed'
moment to pass. We have tried to explain that sex is a gift from God for
marriage and can be fantastic, but he just does not want to hear it!

I fear my baby may never be the same again.

Must go. Are you still coming round for the barbecue tomorrow
evening? We're doing most of our eating outside at the moment.
Saves cleaning the kitchen floor.

Louise

📧 Hi Louise

You know, there are times I'm glad I haven't had children! They're
lovely when they're tiny and you can cuddle them but once they get

to the spotty teen stage you're welcome to them! Looking forward to the BBQ. Love them! It must be the half Canadian in me as I love throwing a steak on the fire and adore a bit of meat with my charcoal.

I can make something if you like. How about that strawberry pavlova/gateau/cake/mousse thing you had when you and Jack came to dinner last week? I think I've mastered it!

Esther

✉ Esther

Did you say mousse or moose? Please don't as I have plenty of cupcakes to eat up! Just bring yourself.

L

PS By the way, yes babies are cute and cuddly if you don't count the smelly nappies, sleepless nights, teething, etc.

🖹 Lou

HA HA HA

Guessing by this that the mousse thing wasn't as great as I thought. You can say it – I won't be offended.

Who else will be coming to the BBQ?

E x

✉ Hi Esther

I have to confess, I have invited Sam. What do you think? Is that OK? And I was thinking of inviting Jacqui too. By the way did I mention that she's going out with a chap called Brian? She met him at the wholesale market over the flour counter. It just goes to show, you never do know what's around the corner. He is a Christian, which is cool. If God has someone for you, you can meet them anywhere, not just in church. So Brian might come to the BBQ as well, and then maybe some of the neighbours.

Just an aside, at one point a few weeks ago, I did wonder if Jacqui had a thing for the 12-year-old at Wendleworth's because every time I saw her in the street she seemed to be carrying a range of shopping bags and I was sure she didn't get through that much food. In the end I realized it was the wrong shop. Turns out she was just finding an excuse to bump into Brian in the wholesale market.

I was thinking of inviting Janette and the kids, but then panicked because it meant we might have to face Garry. Is that terrible? I know it's not my place to forgive him for his infidelity – that's up to Janette – but I just find it so awkward to be around him. He hasn't spoken to me since the communion incident and I'm not sure if he and Janette are reconciled or not. They sit together at church, but perhaps that's just for the girls?

Louise

PS Am saying nothing about the moose!

📧 Hi

All sounds good. You have remembered, haven't you, that I have my sister and family coming for a couple of nights for my birthday weekend and they'll be with me tomorrow – is it still OK to bring them? The boys will love that little blow-up paddling pool. Kai is learning to swim right now and he's loving the water. Kenny Junior looks sweet in his little water wings.

E

DATE: 8 JULY

✉ Dear birthday girl

Looking forward to seeing you and the family.
    Better get organized! I wonder if I can rope in some boys to help?

Louise xx

🖹 Dear Lou

Brilliant! I'm bringing lots of raw stuff and salad. I can do salad.
    Got to say, Naomi and Ken are thrilled and relieved that they don't have to pretend that they enjoy my cooking! We were going to go out for my birthday but the barbecue is a much better idea.
    Ken will also be delighted that he can show his Canadian prowess on the open fire front. As I said, those Canadian men love their charcoaled steak!

E x

 Hi E. Can you drop in to Wendleworth's on your way over please and pick up a few bottles of some non-alcoholic fizzy? I do have that elderflower stuff you like. We seem to have plenty of wine, beer, etc. but nothing for the kids or teetotals. Ta. And Happy Birthday! L

DATE: 9 JULY

🖹 Dear Louise and Jack

May God bless your hospitality and your generous spirit! It was a great day and made the passing of yet another year feel less of a chore – especially after what you had to endure.
    I can't believe you kept the Happy Birthday surprise so well – it must have been killing you. I just thought I was coming round for a

friendly little gathering that just happened to coincide with my big day. I loved the Happy Birthday balloons and banners. Thanks so much! As always, so thoughtful.

After such a wonderful day, I feel 'thanks' is insufficient, so I need to drop round a nice bottle of something for you.

I did get a couple of birthday bottles from both the account managers and one will go away with Ken and Naomi but I don't mind passing the second one on to you. I smiled sweetly, of course, and didn't remind them that they worked for a teetotaller. Colin, as always, came up trumps and brought chocolates.

Lou, what a day! You cruised through it with great panache, although for a moment, when your house group descended en masse, I thought you were going to lose it. I don't think I have ever seen you look quite so confused and pale.

It was like the feeding of the 5,000. After that chilled afternoon in the sunshine I think you rallied very well.

Do you really think they forgot you'd cancelled house group? Or maybe they smelled the grilled sausages and fancied a free meal?

The food was fab. I may not be able to cook but I can appreciate good grub. Naomi, Ken and the boys had a blast. Laurence was so sweet to play with Kenny Jr and Kai all afternoon. The following morning over breakfast Naomi asked, 'Are all your friends so generous?' I wanted to tell her the truth about the 22 unexpected guests but decided it was best to leave her in the dark. I don't think she clocked that most of the evening guests were from YOUR church, not mine.

Every time the doorbell went I wanted to crease up. But I have to say you excelled yourself when your Rev mentioned that we could at least have communion together at the end of the night. Burger buns will take on a new meaning.

The singing was good wasn't it? I especially liked the rendition of 'Happy Birthday' in full four-part harmony. At least the neighbours were there so they couldn't complain about the noise.

There were even enough of the cupcakes to go round. Did you get a premonition that you might be invaded by hoards of hungry house groupers, or did you just get carried away with all the colourful choices of icing options?

The cakes were fantastic and yes, I did guess they were decorated in all the ski jacket colours! I loved them but I think the bright orange, purple and green left a few people a little bemused.

It really was the best birthday party I've had for years, and such a laugh. Thank you. Thank you. Thank you.

And what can I say about your gift? An intensive cooking course is just the thing! I know I've joked about it in the past but actually I do think it will help. I looked up the venue online and the hotel looks fabulous. A real treat of a weekend. It's really kind of you. Thanks SO MUCH! I'll be booking it in the near future and you can be my first dinner guests post course. I hope to have progressed from duck curry with orange bits floating in it.

Hopefully see you very soon – once the family have gone. Thanks for offering to babysit Kai and Ken Jr while we go in to London tomorrow for adult sightseeing. We want to go to some museums as well as the Tower of London and Buckingham Palace, so can we drop them around to yours at about 9.30 a.m.? You're right, a whole day in a hot capital city might not be entirely what little ones are after. And because we'll be able to stay out late, there have also been some hints about a show, which should be fun.

Esther x

DATE: 11 JULY

📧 Dear Lou

Sorry to miss you when we came to pick up the boys after London. They were flat out on the couch, all snuggly with Jack after a long day of fun – and that was just Jack. Wasn't Monday meant to be his 'day off'? Hope the Bible class went well.

Isn't God good? London was great, but we had given up on the idea of the show when we checked the prices. However, we'd just turned the corner at Covent Garden after having lunch when this American chap came up to us and asked if we wanted tickets to a show. At first we thought he might be a ticket tout so we sort of nodded and smiled. He held out three tickets and said he couldn't use them. We went to ask him how much they were but when Ken reached for his wallet, this guy said, 'No – please – they are on me!' And then he vanished.

A London show for free – great seats and three of them! It was even the show I wanted to see! It was a really special treat, a miracle. Do things like that really happen?

God bless the Americans!

Esther x

✉ Dear Esther

God is good – all the time! What a lovely gift. He does surprise us at times, doesn't he?

Next time I visit London I might have to hang around Covent Garden for a bit. Who knows what God might have coming my way? Just mentioned this to Jack and he said, 'Best not to stand around on street corners in London – people might get the wrong idea.'

Thanks for the bottle you left at ours. Jack was in despair at the condition of his wine collection, although I think he is more upset that Rev opened a £45 bottle for the post BBQ communion when he doesn't even drink wine. Jack was pleased he'd hidden it previously as it meant it had survived Bobby's birthday debacle, so for it to then be used for communion was rather difficult for him to accept graciously. I reminded Jack that as an elder he should know that God only wants our best and he growled at me and mumbled what I thought sounded like 'do gooder'!

SO you and Sam looked friendly enough at the barbecue. Anything I should know? Did he give you anything for your birthday?

Lou

☰ Dear L

No – nothing more. Just a friend helping a friend. Naomi also commented, 'He's nice!' but I swore her to secrecy. If my mum found out that Sam was around then it might get back to Harriet, and then to Tom. I'm not ready for that yet. Am I being too sensitive about Tom?

Sam gave me a sweet silver necklace with a maple leaf on it – a nod towards my family connections in Canada. A really thoughtful gift. I hadn't even told him it was my birthday, so I'm guessing that a certain someone who sometimes shares a pew with him at church did the honours before the big day? Thanks again!

Naomi was well impressed with the gift, winked and said something like, 'Just a friend eh?'

I am sooo confused . . .

Esther

DATE: 12 JULY

✉ Dear Esther

I am sure you really do know how you feel. If Sam is 'just a friend' then why would it worry you what Tom heard/thought? Is there something else you are specifically worried about? Come on Esther . . . It was a really thoughtful present. Did it not make you heart skip just a little?

L ☺

☰ Dear Lou

As always, you've hit the nail on the head. But I really don't know how I feel. I'm at sixes and sevens. Don't think I'm still in love with Tom – just don't know if I am ready to move forward yet.

Esther

12

SUBJECT: HOLIDAY TIME

✉ Dear Esther

It is fast approaching September and I wondered if you had
spoken to Sue about the wedding? I know you don't want to go,
particularly watching your newly dyed wedding dress floating down
the aisle on Skinny Sue. I'm still amazed that you not only agreed
to let her have the dress but that you're still thinking about going to
the wedding!

I wondered if you fancied a weekend away? Jack has spare air
miles and has offered them to me. He's been away such a lot recently
and knows I need to get out of here. I didn't know he had been saving
them but he wants me to have them and suggested that a shopping
trip to New York might be good. He said that if I made him go with
me he'd only slow me down, so he suggested you and I can do some
early Christmas shopping and maybe even get some bargains. My
husband is so lovely at times.

So, what do you say? It would be something amazing to look
forward to. I love travelling and have never been to New York. I want
to try some authentic New York cheesecake! The food in the city is
meant to be great.

Here's something to make you smile. You remember Chris, the
chap that looks like a hippie in our church? On Sunday evening we
had some nostalgic moments when our Rev decided that we should
sing some of the choruses that came out the Ark.

Chris was sitting in front of me singing loudly and out of tune and I suddenly realized that he was singing, 'Soon and very soon we are going to the moon.'

Trying to be discreet, I asked him why he was singing those words with such enthusiasm. 'Aren't we going to the moon then when Jesus comes back?' he asked. I cannot remember much of the service and I doubt he can, but we both know that space landings aren't in our future. I hope.

So speak soon and very soon . . . unless you are off to the moon.

Let me know about NY NY!

A very excited Louise

▱ Dear, dear Louise

YOU ARE AN AMAZING FRIEND! New York would be fantastic!! Let's do it! Please thank Jack too. I've only been once and that was when I was a student and stayed in a downtown, rather grubby backpackers' hostel. I had a fabulous time – apart from the bed bugs . . .

I've turned down the offer of Sue and Ron's wedding. Having given them not only my wedding date but also the dress, I really can't face actually being there. Seeing that lovely dress dyed cream . . . I think not.

Esther xxx

PS Re New York: are you going to look up some deals online? Shall I come round so we can talk? I want to pay for the hotel if you get the air tickets.

DATE: 14 AUGUST

✉ Hi Esther

Why don't you come round for coffee, say Saturday? The boys will be out. Aunty Charise has a new man in her life – I think she said his name is Duncan. And they're taking our brood for the day! Getting them out of our hair before Jack and I take them off on the family holiday. So I've got a bit of time to plough through online offers!

By the way, have you really decided not to take a summer break this year? Will going to see your mum and family be enough of a holiday?

Louise

DATE: 20 AUGUST

🖃 Dear Louise

Thanks for arranging the NY thing. October can't come quickly enough. I can't believe we got the whole trip – flights AND hotel – on the air miles. Leaves us loads of cash for shopping.

I need to go and see Mum and also pop down to Naomi and Ken and the kids, and I can't be away from the office for any length of time at the moment. However, I'm going to Cornwall the day after tomorrow to work on that holiday business contract I've told you about. I hope the weather improves because the forecast looks dismal. They have a photo shoot for next year's summer brochure and I really should be there to ensure the photographers get all the right shots, so I might take a few days on the coast while I'm away! I also need to factor some time in for that cookery course you gave me, although I went on the website yesterday and it's such a popular course that I may not get on until next year. It looks really good and I think it's time I really learned to cook rather than making do with salads, soups and microwave meals.

As for 'away' holidays it all gets so expensive. When WILL holiday companies start to treat us 'single travellers' more fairly? Out of interest, I was looking at some offers on a cruise the other day and the 'single supplement' pretty much doubled the cost. I don't want to have to share a cabin with some unknown female who snores. And I have no one who I want to drag along and whose friendship I risk losing because they discover that I snore! Sorry to tell you that, but at least it won't be a surprise when we share that lovely room overlooking Central Park.

And I really don't fancy those 'Christian singles' holidays that everyone goes on about. Did you know that Sam is going on one this month? He let this slip when I saw him for coffee the other day – yes, we met for coffee, although it was still NOT A DATE!

He'll be on a bus with a group of other Christians travelling to Spain where they will spend a week in a monastery. Apparently, or so he says, he was persuaded to go by the Rev at your church. A group are going.

Talking of church friends ... well you saw MY surprise when Charise returned with the boys yesterday. Her Duncan is the Duncan at Rivers of Life – our organist, the one who was chased by the whole of the Christian female population of the region when his last relationship broke up. I was wondering why he's been looking so happy recently. At church last week instead of the usual 'God be with you till we meet again' at the end of the service he played 'Shine Jesus Shine' followed by an excellent rendition of 'Walking on Sunshine'. . .

Have a great holiday!

Esther x

DATE: 24 AUGUST

✉ Dear Esther

Am sitting here by the pool with a book, cheap and nice-tasting wine in our rented French gite and it's glorious. It must be nearly 30 °C!

I am glad you managed a few days off in Cornwall but sorry about the downpours. Incredible that the moment Jack leaves his garden it starts to rain. He has been worrying about the lawn all summer. Personally, I think we should have it Astro Turfed. The boys are always playing football on it and that leaves it patchy and often bare.

Although we're having a wonderful time, Jack keeps worrying about what might be happening to his lawn now that he's not there to tend it and manicure it. I told him it needs plastic surgery, not a manicure!

When did my husband become so fastidious? I thought that sort of thing was meant to be a sign of 'old age' but he's got early onset 'obsessions'.

Anyway, the boys are having a fine time. Ollie, who we had to prise away from his Chloe, now appears to be skirting around a certain young French woman who serves in the local patisserie. Her name is Valerie and she's a minx. A little bit too buxom for our liking and a couple of years Oliver's senior. I didn't think I'd say it but . . . come back Chloe, all is forgiven!

Bobby, too, has a little friend. She's Welsh and is also staying with her family on holiday here. Megs is what she calls herself. Sweet.

Laurence has buddied up with a group of lads from the local village and they spend most of their time riding bikes and dive-bombing in the pool, which is strictly prohibited. Not a girl in sight, fortunately. It won't be long though. The blow-up bed trauma is long gone!

Must go. Breakfast croissants call!

L

PS I am still keeping up the diet. I got into that new top we bought in the Spring sales and it looks lovely. A whole two sizes smaller than I was wearing last year. Thanks for your support!

📧 Dear Lou

WOW! Well done on the new top. Before you know it you'll be having to rush out for a new bikini! Hope you're also finding the floppy hat useful. Don't get sunburnt.

E

✉ Esther

Me in a BIKINI?
    No matter HOW thin I get I don't think that will ever happen again.

L

🖃 Louise

Never say never.

E

13 ≣✉

SUBJECT: SAD NEWS

DATE: 17 SEPTEMBER

✉ Dear Louise

Thanks SO much for yesterday. Perhaps only you and my mum and sister really understood how much I was dreading it. I know I wanted to do something completely different to take my mind off my non-nuptials but I didn't expect a trip on the London Eye!

It was amazing. Thanks!

OK, so I didn't quite manage to forget that at 2 p.m., just when we were 'taking off', Sue was prancing down MY aisle in MY dress (albeit dyed off-white) but you really helped ease the pain. Thanks for putting up with the tears.

What a fabulous day it was. I love Covent Garden and just to be there in the early Autumn sunshine was brilliant. I've often hankered after running a bit of a market stall and I just find snooping around the CG offerings a really relaxing experience. That and the 'all you can eat' Chinese buffet in China Town . . . You know what I like!

I wasn't going to go to church this morning – didn't fancy all the 'poor old Esther' side glances. But I woke up early (chow mein still rumbling) and I decided to front the congregation. I'm glad I did.

Yes, I had to see Ron and Sue's flowers still up in church and hear some reports of what apparently was quite a 'nice' day. Rev T had to rescue me from a couple of older women who were intent on 'consoling' me with well meant but inappropriate sympathies, but I managed the morning.

Enough of that though.

Really just wrote to say thanks and to pass on some sad news.

The blessed Angela has gone to meet the angels.

Rev Tracey announced it in church today. Apparently she died on Friday night.

I feel so sorry for POG What will he do? He relied on his Ange! And I feel a bit guilty now for being cross and critical about her. And a little bit guilty because I was feeling so sorry for myself and I only lost a marriage, not a lifelong partner!

Esther

DATE: 18 SEPTEMBER

✉ Hi Esther

Sorry to hear about Angela. That's sad. I also feel a bit guilty now about my earlier prayer for release for POG from domestic bondage! Sometimes I say things and I know you know I am really joking but what would other people say if they read what I have written? I must sound awful sometimes. I do moan a lot!

How is POG? Please let me know when the funeral is. I really would like to go. I feel awful for him. Can you send me his address? Shall I send flowers? What do you send men? Not sure what the protocol is. Maybe I will ask Jason the Florist.

Lou

PS Don't feel guilty for feeling sad on Saturday. Glad to help you through it! Always wanted to do the London Eye and Jack and I thought it would be a great experience for you.

 Hi Lou. Funeral is on Friday. I'll get you the address. E

✉ Dear Esther

What did you think of the flowers we sent for Angela's funeral? I
spoke to Jason. I actually went into the shop. Didn't take Jack along.
Jason was really helpful. He suggested those white carnations. They
had some lovely large ones.

Now . . . not being one to gossip (much) but . . . does POG have
a sister? I popped into the post office this morning and he seemed
quite chummy with the outgoing brunette behind the counter. I did
not see her at the funeral and I can't say I've see her in the post office
before, but the memory plays tricks especially when you have low
blood sugars. Pounds for Africa is benefitting from my struggle at
the moment. Also think I would benefit from a deep cleanse to the
system. Did I type that? Maybe not what you want to hear.

Please do remind me when I get old – I do not want a cremation.
Even though the sun was bright, it was so cold in that chapel. Seeing
the curtains close and hearing the motors go wasn't nice. The engines
did not seem to stop. They could really do with some oil. I wonder if
they do oil them?

I don't know why I got so upset at the funeral. Strange really
because I didn't know Angela that well – must be those hormones. I
think any funeral or cremation also reminds you of previous ones you
have been to and I have to say, the memories of my granny's funeral
came flooding back. That was a very sad day for me, even though I
knew she had gone to heaven, the 13-year-old me was just absolutely
devastated. She was such a wonderful woman and such an important
part of my childhood.

Jack knew it was a bad day for me and decided to make me
less stressed and morose over the coffee and biscuits (was that the
'Wake'? Not very 'awakening' . . .). He told me a story about the
last crem he went to. The minister got his finger stuck in the button
to release the coffin. Jack was wondering why the minister was so
enthusiastic about singing the last hymn twice and telling everyone to

sing it out loud when he saw him trying to release his finger! That's why you might have noticed us laughing hysterically in the corner. It was either that, or cry. Hope POG didn't see us as it was a bit disrespectful.

I always thought that Angela was quite a focal point at Rivers of Life. Hadn't she and Geoff been members for ever? That's what I was always led to believe. Ever since she's been on my radar (and not just what you've reported) she seems to have been involved in every aspect of life at Rivers. So I was very surprised at how few people attended her funeral. Wasn't she on the flower, tea and coffee rota, reception, welcoming and communion set-up?

I am so glad we went to her funeral but it was 'peculiar', as you said, being virtually the only ones in the congregation who knew the hymns, or at least were prepared to sing out loud. I've experienced this at weddings and funerals and christenings when the majority of attendees are 'non churchgoers' but you just don't expect that at the funeral of a 'lifelong Christian', as she was described.

Mind you, Rev T has got a good set of lungs, hasn't she? Thank goodness she can carry a good tune. But I was astonished to see Father Sean at the organ. Where was Duncan? Isn't he your usual organist? I'm suspecting that the no show at the funeral proves that the blessed Angela did, unfortunately, upset a lot of people in her lifetime. So sad.

I wonder if not having children made her angry at God, which resulted in her being an angry person generally? Geoff seems so different in character. So mild-mannered and inoffensive.

Louise

DATE: 26 SEPTEMBER

✉ Dear Lou

I promise I won't let you be cremated! But I can't understand you because it's so economical – at least that, apparently, is what

Angela said to Poor Old Geoff. That's why she was sprinkled on the rose bushes at the crem. No need to maintain a gravestone. POG explained all this to me after church on Sunday.

Yes, Angela was on every conceivable church committee. She was in charge of the refreshments team, chaired the flower committee, was involved in the women's aid group and much, much more. I think the only thing she didn't get involved in was the youth work. I believe she aspired to be a good person and probably was a great person, and a sympathetic Christian, but unfortunately she didn't have that 'off switch' between brain and mouth so she didn't manage to show it. Angela was very 'direct' (I think that's what Rev T said in the eulogy?). Unfortunately she rather dominated proceedings wherever she put in an appearance and I'm afraid that showed in the congregation at her last church service!

As for Duncan, he's such a lovely person but even he was her victim. He let it slip once that he was avoiding Angela. Apparently she nabbed him one Sunday morning – yes, you've guessed it, during after-church coffee, her hunting ground of choice. Apparently the conversation went something like this:

'Duncan. You're a nice young man. Why aren't you married?'

Angela certainly had the knack of getting to the point. No foreplay for her. Oh, the thought of that makes me feel slightly queasy.

Duncan was a little taken aback and mumbled something like, 'Well, er . . . not met the right one,' etc.

You'll never guess what Angela then came out with!

'You know, Geoff and I were watching television the other night and we saw this really interesting documentary about men and relationships. It's awfully confusing, isn't it? Not like when Geoff and I met and fell in love.'

I know that sort of caught me off-guard as well. Anyway, to continue, Angela ploughed on:

'We saw this man on the TV and he was very attractive. Just the sort that girls would go for, I'm sure. But he turned out to be . . . you know . . .'

Duncan said at this point Angela cocked her head sort of knowingly, and so he dived in with, 'Engaged? Married? Divorced?'

Angela then lowered her voice and spoke deliberately but rather conspiratorially, looking Duncan straight in the eye, 'No, Duncan. He was, you know, the other way inclined . . . if you know what I mean.'

She then waited for a response. Duncan said he just stared at her in disbelief, speechless. Angela carried on relentlessly, in the same whispering kind of 'don't worry I won't tell anyone if you fess up' sort of tone.

'You know Duncan . . . if you are . . . you know . . . then . . . you will need to stay celibate. You do know that, don't you? So . . . do you . . . are you?'

Duncan, I'm glad to report, did not shout out loud, 'How dare you, you old windbag. My sexuality is MY business. No I'm NOT GAY! And even if I were it's none of your business!' As he told me, he realized that if he did so she'd probably go home to POG and report, 'That Duncan . . . he protesteth too strongly . . . and you KNOW what that means Geoff.' Before long, he feared, the town would be overrun with rumours that the organist at Rivers of Life is . . . you know . . . one of those 'special gentlemen'.

So instead of losing it, Duncan just quietly and sensibly addressed his nemesis:

'Well, Angela. Please be assured that I am not homosexual. If I was I would not be ashamed of it and I would sort out my relationship with God myself. However, meanwhile, I keep looking for Miss Right, hoping that when I meet her I will have the sort of relationship that I'm sure you and Geoff started out wanting to have when, as you said, you were in the first flush of youth and love.'

Classic, I thought.

Angela was, for once, struck dumb. I'm not sure she understood exactly what Duncan was alluding to vis-à-vis the 'relationship' that Angela and POG had descended into over the years – at least what the world perceived they had drifted into.

But I think that explains why Duncan just happened to be out of town on funeral day. He is a very nice young man and not nasty at all, but I know he always avoided her after that Sunday morning and I'd like to think it was a coincidence that he forgot to sort out a replacement on the organ for her farewell service. Being there might have made him feel a bit of a hypocrite. Which is, truth be told, exactly how I felt!

Thank God for Father Sean. It was a bit odd to have a Catholic priest presiding over the music but it goes to show what a great friend he is to the church – and Rev Tracey!

Anyway, I don't think POG noticed the organist snub – hope not. I felt so sorry for him at the funeral with his little band of friends. I think they might be golf-related buddies (I overheard talk of 'handicaps' at the wake, which I presume was golf-related) although I've no idea when Angela let him loose on the links.

I wondered if Geoff would be at church so soon after the funeral, but he turned up and was smothered with love by all the older ladies. Trying to think whether the post office clerk might have been among them, but I'm sure all the women on the refreshments team are retired, so she can't be. I'll give it some thought.

Esther xx

PS Thought the flowers were lovely!

DATE: 27 SEPTEMBER

🖃 Hi Lou

Just got in from a choir practice and had to report something really strange and rather worrying.

It's POG – the grieving hasn't lasted long.

Angela is barely cold in the grave – or whatever it is when one is cremated – and POG appears to be a changed man. Everyone at church thought he'd buckle and crumble once he didn't have Angela to order him around. But far from it! He's ditched the blue anorak, has had a haircut and seems to have acquired new specs. He's taken to wearing aftershave and has a slight swing in his step.

How do I know he's wearing Brut now? I'm going to tell you something and you need to swear to secrecy. Not even Jack ... promise? He cornered me after choir tonight and ... asked me out! I was mortified. He must be 75 if he's a day! And he only buried his wife last week!

But it gets better. Apparently, he confided in me, just a few weeks before the blessed Angela shuffled off her mortal coil, she said to POG, 'If I go before you, Geoffrey, I want you to marry again. You're useless on your own and you need someone to take care of you. Esther is desperate to marry, and she'll look after you. So marry her!'

After all that 'God wants you to remain single to do his work' stuff, suddenly Angela realized that perhaps doing God's will would involve me looking after her husband!

I had no idea how to respond to the newly bereaved Geoff. I declined as politely as I could and headed for the exit.

What have I done to deserve this?

E xxx

✉ Hi Esther

Bless him! Poor Old Geoff!
  Sorry to say but Jack and I are in stitches here!

Lou xxxxx

🖃 Dear Louise

Glad I could be the cause of such jollity in your household! I know you share pretty much everything with Jack so I'll forgive you on this occasion for revealing my sordid little secret – but I'm trusting you both to keep the joke in-house!

Esther

PS – I think I need to get out more. ☺

✉ Dear Esther

Our lips are sealed. Sorry, but Jack caught me giggling over the
laptop and before I knew it I had spilled the beans. I'd be absolutely
no good under interrogation.

Lou xx

DATE: 30 SEPTEMBER

✉ Dear Esther

Let's try and catch up soon. Need to finalize details on our NY break
– can't wait!

Life is hectic at the moment – for some reason a few of my regular
clients have cancelled their orders and I'm desperately trying to
rebuild some business. Thanks for your help with the website, by the
way. And it WOULD be good to set up a Lou's Cupcakes Twitter
account but I don't know where to start. Anything you could do
would be massively helpful.

I've also got Darcy coming tomorrow. I must make up the bed in
the spare room. Darcy is so fussy about how many pillows she has,
and the tog value of the duvet. She is allergic to feathers so no feather
pillows either. I have a Darcy box in the attic containing all the stuff
she requests when she stays. I have a couple of those awful towel
sets she gave us in there so I'll bring those out so she'll think we use
them. Jack thinks I am mad but it helps keep the peace. Jack says it's
like having a film star staying.

Lou x

14

SUBJECT: THE WICKED STEPSISTER

DATE: 4 OCTOBER

✉ Dear Esther

Sorry I have not been around. As you will remember I have Darcy staying – aka the wicked stepsister. I got the spare bedroom all ready for her and forgot to put in the alarm clock, a water jug and a mat. She was not happy. I really think she must have some problem. She makes it so hard for people to like her. She is always making comments. The boys are on their best behaviour – and bribed.

I was telling her what happened at the first aid course and she just laughed. I did not want someone laughing. I needed some TLC So instead, I am sneaking in an email to you while Darcy is doing some yoga thing. That's why she needed a mat!

Lou

✉ Dear Louise

I forgot Darcy was staying. How long is she with you? You can always bring her round for coffee to give you a break from the stress of having to deal with her yourself.

I promise I won't laugh. What happened at the first aid course?

Esther

✉ Hi E

OK, here goes. I told you I wasn't keen on that course but I know it's a good thing to have. You never know when you will need first aid skills. Really handy in the kitchen if someone has an accident with a knife or burns themselves, not to mention sorting out teenagers' bumps and bruises.

I really should have done something like it years ago. Did I tell you I once had to do that 'hymn lick' manoeuvre on Laurence when a sweet went down the wrong way? He was laughing so much at something that had happened.

Anyway, with a resolve to be a better person and all that, off I trundled to the community centre. The instructor is a neighbour of one of the elders in church so I presumed all would be well.

There were lots of introductions and the first hour went fast. Lots of talking about things such as treating burns and cuts. We learned how to put on a simple bandage and how to make a sling out of a scarf. Very helpful, and interesting.

But the second hour was awful. We got to the part of the course that was all about managing someone who is unconscious and we needed to learn what position to place them in so they would be safe. The very friendly instructor suggested I could be the patient. I had to lie on the ground just slumped 'unconscious'. He was telling everyone what to do and had to push me into the 'recovery position'. He made some loud comment along the lines of 'obviously heavy people can be difficult to move'. I was very pleased that I'd worn trousers to the event and I wanted to scream, 'Actually, a couple of months ago I couldn't get into these and now, look, they are quite baggy!' But even if I'd had the guts to do so I did not have a chance. As he attempted to manipulate me into the recovery position, he turned badly and put his back out. Ironic really.

So there we all were, waiting in the community centre for the ambulance. I was mortified at the comments he had made, and felt I was the one who deserved the sweetened tea – not the instructor. A couple of people in the class seemed to imply that if I hadn't been such an elephant it would not have happened. Talk about a pounding to one's self-esteem . . .

Lou

▤ **Dear Lou**

YOU ARE NOT TO BLAME! Forget them!

E x

✉ Dear Esther

Thank you. I think it's worse as I have Darcy staying. She had no sympathy for me. Didn't say anything comforting. Just laughed. I love her, but she really doesn't make it easy.

On Monday I took her out to Clethorpes House – you know, that lovely National Trust house we provide the cupcakes for? I get a discounted entrance rate. Anyway we bumped into Jacqui doing one of our deliveries and I introduced her to Darcy. Jacqui greeted her with the usual pleasantries and said, 'You really don't look like sisters,' to which Darcy replied, with attitude I might add, 'Well that's because I am her stepsister.'

Poor Jacqui, she didn't know where to put herself. I felt so sorry for her. There was an awkward silence and then Darcy stormed off. Sometimes I think she doesn't want to be my sister and she is rather annoyed that she is. I did have a lump in my throat. Jacqui was lovely about it. Thank God for friends!

So I made a huge decision – why should I put up with Darcy being rude to my friends? After an interesting drive home, accompanied by Matt Redman on a CD and a silent stepsister, I decided to challenge her. I waited until we got home. Then once in the kitchen the conversation went like this:

Me: 'Darcy, why do you make such a habit of being rude to my friends?'

Darcy: 'I know you only have me to stay out of some forced feeling of duty. You never wanted me to be your sister.'

Me: 'You know that's not true' (fingers crossed, slight white lie, thinking of the room requests).

Darcy: 'You are so happy with this great home, family, Jack and your business. You don't want me here too.'

Me: 'There is always room for you, Darcy. My life may look great but I still have my struggles and hassles.'

Darcy (slim, Katie Holmes-lookalike with fab job): 'But you are happy!'

She started bawling her eyes out, at which point Jack entered the room and swiftly turned round and left again. He mouthed, 'What's wrong?' I just smiled.

After an in-depth counselling session (glad I did that Christian care and counselling course all those years ago and, most importantly, that I still remember some of the basic principles), during which she admitted all sorts of jealousies over many years, I am very glad to say we have started to lay foundations for a better relationship. My maybe-not-so-wicked stepsister hugged me and apologized for being so sharp with people. She is quite an unhappy little person really. I didn't realize. I've been so obsessed with my own dislike for her silly little ways, her pettiness and her nastiness, I had no idea she was such a sad person. She's even jealous of my faith, and I ended up reminding her that she, too, can have a great relationship with Jesus and that if she put her hand in his, life would be better, I am sure.

I think God has been at work this week at No. 22 Arkland Street.

L

DATE: 5 OCTOBER

🖃 Hi Louise

So pleased you're sorting things out with Darcy. Fantastic. What an answer to prayer. I know I'm lucky having Naomi as my lovely little sister. I can't count the number of times she's been there for me. I'd be devastated if I could not see her and Mum and other family members. Family is important even if you can't stand them some of the time. Even if you don't always like them, you can always love them.

Remember that next time you're breaking up World War 3 between Oliver, Bobby and Laurence! At some point in time they'll realize they love each other even if right now they can't stand the sight of their siblings.

I am so glad that God is on Darcy's case.

Talking of cases, we'll soon be in NY NY living it up! Can't wait . . . Macy's and Bloomingdales here we come! I'm also hoping to get us some Broadway tickets for our second night as a thank you for all your support during the Tom situation. Watch this space.

Is Jack able to take us to the airport?

Esther xxx

📧 Hi again

Forgot to say . . . you know you saw POG being friendly with the woman in the post office? It appears, even though I spurned his attentions, he's undeterred in his quest to find another true love. The brunette is a person called Margaret. She does go to our church – her husband died a couple of years ago.

She turned up at choir practice tonight – it's the first time I've seen her there and I saw Geoff wink at her (yes – the mind boggles I know). The women sitting in front of me saw it too and tutted disapprovingly.

After choir I did a little detective work and discovered that, indeed, Margaret recently took on a part-time counter clerk job in the post office.

So . . . mystery solved. POG is a mourning widower no longer.

In a strange, perverted way I feel rather rejected. Geoff wasn't interested in me at all, he just wants a woman. I guess some men just can't stand to be alone.

Sigh . . . Esther

✉ Dear Esther

You definitely need that break in New York if you're pining after a 75-year-old, recently widowed man who smells of Brut.

L ☺

DATE: 10 OCTOBER

✉ Hi Esther

Tried to phone but didn't get through. I will phone later if I don't get a reply. I am so looking forward to the trip. I feel like I have had my case packed for weeks. Actually I think possibly I have had. Jack has tripped over it twice on the way to the en suite.

I am gabbling! I just really can't wait. It'll be bliss just to be out of the house and not crawling over muddy boots and socks. It does really feel like a laundry in our house at times. I am sure our washing breeds while it's in the washing basket.

Airport plans have changed though. Jack is busy – that contract is a killer. But I happened to mention our trip to Sam last Sunday and he's offered. ☺ We might have to squeeze into the front seat of his van (bags me the window seat) but it saves the taxi fare. You can squeeze up to Sam.

L

🖥 LOUISE LOUISE LOUISE

You little rascal. You're so transparent! ☺

✉ Dear E

You're welcome – what are friends for?

L

15

SUBJECT: THE CITY THAT NEVER SLEEPS

✉ Dear Jack

We are having an AMAZING time. We really MUST come here together sometime in the next few years. Maybe come for one of the parades? I am loving being here, but am missing you. I know I have already phoned you twice – I won't do so again unless it is an emergency.

On the flight over Esther had to prod me to stop me snoring at one point, but we had such a laugh. I think all the running around before leaving home was too much. Next time, remind me not to take any last-minute cake orders. I am sure I mixed some up.

The taxi ride into the city was mad. I'm sure the taxi driver took us the 'long way' but we got to the hotel in one piece. Our place is right in the centre of the city.

I hope you are managing the boys and keeping up with their schedules. Remember to check the fridge if you aren't sure of anything. It should be easy for you – like project managing! Did you remember Bobby's dental appointment yesterday? Don't forget I left loads of food in the freezer. There are also a couple of fruitcakes in the pantry. How long did those cupcakes I left you last?!

The hotel is great. Even though it is at the cheaper end of the market, it's very comfortable and good value. I didn't realize how close to everything we would be. The only down side is that there is a huge Southern Baptist conference in the building next door and people keep trying to herd us into it. I think we must have a 'Christian' look about us. Esther is threatening to wear a miniskirt and glittery top with plunging neckline to put them off the scent.

However, I don't think we were helped on our first day when we were spotted walking through reception. Esther's suitcase is covered in 'I Love Jesus' stickers. She says it is a throwback to her 'I want everyone to know I am a Christian and then they will get converted' days. She tells me that this is the luggage she takes on her 'holidays' as opposed to her 'business trips'! She reckons no one will risk the wrath of God by stealing it. I told her it is weird and she needed to join the 21st century and get a bag that rolls on wheels.

Twice so far I have had to fake needing the loo and escape through a side door to avoid getting cornered by the Southern Baptists and steered into the conference. They are all camped in our hotel. Another day of it and we may need to move accommodation!

The Empire State Building is enormous! My feet are sore from all the walking but I am hopeful that the exercise will balance out the amount I am eating. I think we should bring the boys here as we will definitely be able to fill them up. No more moaning about being hungry!

I have managed to get their pressies. We called in to Macy's and I got a good deal on some sports gear. I promise I have not spent a fortune. Hopefully off to see a show tonight – Esther has promised to treat me so we are going to try and get tickets. Kind, isn't she?

Love you so much.

Louise xxxxxx

📧 Dear Mum

I really must bring you here. It's fab! You really would love it. We are having such a hoot, mainly at the expense of the Southern Baptist women's conference members who are in our hotel and attending their church conference next door. I bet you never expected me to say that! Why, Lord, did you place us here?

The hotel is actually rather good. They have a fantastic buffet breakfast that finishes just before lunch. Louise thinks we could go in for breakfast and lunch. She's always thinking of money-saving tips! I thought we'd have to share but we each have a lovely room with a 'Jack and Jill' bathroom (or, as Lou insists, a 'Jack and Louise' bathroom) in between.

We've already been up the Empire State Building and seen The Rockettes. They were cool. We had a fantastic time at Macy's and are off to Bloomingdales tomorrow. We're hoping to go for a horse-drawn carriage ride around Central Park to enjoy the colours. The trees are just turning and it's spectacular.

I've eaten a lot! The New York cheesecake is to die for. Louise has been asking all the dinner chefs for their recipes.

Hope you're well. Will email when I get back.

Much love

Esther x

Date: 16 October

 Jack, what do you mean I am like my fruitcake? Anyway, panic over. Long story but God has looked after us – did we ever doubt he would? Lou x

 Jack, we have landed!! So looking forward to seeing you. Where are you parked? L x

 Sam – am back from NY. Catch up soon? Esther

DATE: 17 OCTOBER

🖃 Dear Mum

We're back safely and I take back everything I said about the Baptists!

Before we left the hotel, the Southern Baptist women's conference swung into gear. They had heard at reception that we had 'lost' our luggage. As we'd checked out of our room we had to leave our bags in a 'holding area' near reception and, after a morning in the city, we returned to the hotel to retrieve our bags and catch a taxi out to the airport only to find that our two main bags were gone!

The hotel staff weren't sure what had happened. They were adamant that they could not have been stolen, but thought perhaps someone else had taken them by mistake. Why anyone would take an old-style suitcase with 'I Love Jesus' stickers on it 'by mistake' is a mystery to me. It's why I leave the stickers on the bag . . . a sort of holy 'anti-theft' device . . . I always think that if a thief sees that bag they'll think, 'Not worth stealing – will be full of Bibles.'

Anyway, the hotel have promised to try to track them down. Given that they contained most of the presents we'd bought, and some of the new clothes we'd managed to pick up, Lou and I are praying hard for that.

Meanwhile, the Southern Baptist sisterhood stepped up to help. Between us, we ended up being given more money than we went with and two shopping bags of 'gifts' that included various items of clothing (a few frilly shirts and floral skirts that you can have, if you like. They're not really Lou's or my style). Curiously we also acquired some interesting hand-knitted items – some hats and scarfs, and what we think may be half a dozen knitted dish cloths. We're not sure what the Southern Baptist women usually get up to during their conferences but this one obviously included a crafts workshop. Actually some of the handmade items are exquisite,

The lovely, generous women just would not stop giving us things, even though we did try to stem the tide of gifts. Lou has suggested that we do a craft sale now we're back!

The ladies were so kind and didn't want us to have a bad opinion of the States. And they were also super excited that we are Christians.

I am just amazed by God's blessing on us, and so glad that we had our passports, etc. in our handbags and not with the main luggage. What a headache that would have been.

Speak soon and looking forward to seeing you this weekend.

Esther x

DATE: 20 OCTOBER

✉ Dear Esther

Just heard from the NY hotel. They've tracked down my bag but are still trying to locate yours. Apparently one of the porters has been taking his job description literally – the hotel has discovered that he's been 'portering' cases away over quite a period. The police found my bag in his apartment, along with several dozen more, unopened and untouched. I give thanks that Jack's sense of security is quite so intense and he persuaded me to take the strong-box suitcase.

'It's like Fort Knox! No one will get into it without the keys!' he always says. He's right!

Anyway, praying that your bag will turn up.

Meanwhile, even though we booked on air miles, the hotel have refunded me the whole cost of the hotel stay by way of a 'goodwill gesture'. How amazing is that? I was worrying that I might not be able to pay some of the bills this month (business still not great – I guess people cut back on luxuries like cupcakes when things are tight). God is amazing, isn't he!

And, what with all the cash those lovely Baptist ladies forced upon us, we've come out of this better than we started – well apart from your still missing bag and all its contents.

Lou

📧 Dear Louise

I fear my 'I Love Jesus' bag has disappeared for good. The hotel
has offered me compensation for the loss of some items but I'm
considering claiming from the insurance.

Not sure how the insurers will react to my description of the
lost/stolen bag: 'Covered in "I Love Jesus" stickers' will probably give
them a laugh! The fear of God's wrath was obviously not enough for
the petty thief who is now enjoying it.

I'm just praying that whoever has acquired my beloved bag will
feel guilt and shame when they realize that it was STOLEN from a
Christ-lover!

Esther

PS That bag has travelled the world with me over the years. Sad to
see it go.

📧 Dear Lou

I've changed my prayer. I've 'released' the 'I Love Jesus' bag to his will.
Am hoping now that God will work a miracle in its new owner. It
contained my Bible and daily reading book, in addition to my clothes
(old and new) and all the pressies.

Praying that the new 'owner' will read that Bible and be saved.

E x

PS I needed to part with the past once and for all, and, in an obscure
and mysterious way, losing the bag has done it. It was a thing of the
past – just like Tom – and now I feel liberated. Happy memories, but I
don't need it to move forward.

✉ Dear Esther

So sorry the bag is gone for good. But amazing that its loss has
'freed' you – at last!

God works in mysterious ways his wonders to perform!

Lots of prayers

Louise

16

SUBJECT: DIFFERENT PLANETS

DATE: 24 OCTOBER

Dear Louise

Work is absolutely mad. Colin is on holiday and I realize I'm lost without him and his pure efficiency.

I'm now faced with TWO preggers account managers. You know the 'new' girl announced she was 'expecting' almost as soon as she stepped over the threshold – now the other married one is also in the family way – again! I'm sure that I'm breaking every HR rule when I say that I'm now hoping that she decides not to return after spawning her FOURTH child! That would solve all my problems. I could upgrade Colin once and for all. Actually I'm thinking of doing that anyway, and making him deputy manager. But I suppose it would be wrong to pray into that pregnant lady situation?

I know I'm a bit of an old moan at the moment – I always seem to be offloading my misery – hope you don't mind. Do say when it gets tiresome, but I can't express myself to many other people without feeling like I'm being judged.

With the 'almost wedding day' now well and truly behind me, and this new 'released' feeling that hasn't yet gone away, I'm beginning to be aware once again of the plight of Christian singles.

Back before Tom, as you know, I really struggled with being single but I have to admit it didn't take long when one became two that I clean forgot what it was like being a singleton – in church and in the 'world' and the pain and the sorrow that brings. Perhaps that's part of the problem – when you have someone you can't imagine being on your own ever again.

This time round, though, I'm a couple of years older and I'm giving my single status a great deal more reflection.

Some things haven't changed. I'm still expected, like all Christian singles, to grin and bear it – well at least smile meekly and accept my situation and, most importantly, to be happy with it.

But this time it's different!

While I accept my situation (what else can I do?) I'm no longer prepared to put up with the attitudes of those around me. Yes, if God requires me to be single, then he will help me through this. I'm not just saying that. I really have to believe it. I do believe it.

But I don't have to put up with all the platitudes and 'teaching' that disregards my feelings as a single.

Do 'marrieds' in church really know what we're going through? Or are marrieds and singles (like in that book *Men Are from Mars, Women Are from Venus*) actually from different planets … no different universes?

Take last Saturday. I was at the Rivers of Life Autumn mixer. Last year I was there with Tom, and although he was like a fish out of water – him not being a Christian and all – I was at least in a 'couple', had someone to get me drinks so I wouldn't have to put up with all the pushing and shoving at the (non-alcoholic) punch bowl, and someone to buddy up with during the country dancing part of the evening. That part is always a bit hideous for those alone – standing/sitting in the corner either hoping to be picked by the only good-looking bloke in the room, or attempting to hide from the guy who you just KNOW is slinking across the room towards you and who you have already politely declined five times during the evening.

As usual for the mixer, pretty much the whole church was present and I felt like a pariah. I wasn't the only single there, I know. But I think the fact that I didn't get married as planned (and previously announced with great celebration), and that Sue and Ron were there showing off their honeymoon tans, which are still intact, emphasized my status.

BTW they MUST have had their tan topped up – no one stays brown for a month and more after a holiday, do they? Well I don't.

Anyway, after the evening not even Rev T could cheer me up. Even she had a 'date' – Father Sean! If I didn't know better I could swear there was something going on there.

But the evening made me realize some fundamental facts of single life.

Some married women are scared of us singles, I think, or at least are very cautious around us. Like they think we're about to run off with their hubbies at the first opportunity, when in truth, I'm just as likely to want to cuddle up next to Frank (slight paunch, halitosis) as I am to run off to Lapland with Santa Claus!

The men? Well, some of them are flirtatious and that's a worry. Others just want to be 'friends' but are not sure the little wife will approve. I'm not going to go into the whole 'can men and women really be friends without sex coming into it?' dilemma (*When Harry Met Sally* – what a great film!) but it is an interesting question.

How do we, as grown-up, usually sane Christians, make friends with members of the opposite sex, married or not, without people thinking that we're (1) doing it (2) wanting to do it or (3) thinking about doing it?

Why is it that church people seem so obsessed with sex that we can't contemplate that people can be 'friends' without wanting to go behind the bike shed for a bit of how's your father?

How, for instance, as a married woman, do you react to the single (or even married) girl who you see Jack laughing with over the tea urn at the back of church after the morning service? Do you get jealous? Do you suspect her motives?

Should I avoid all married men at all costs just so I don't make their wives feel uncomfortable?

So many questions – so few answers.

But it IS just after midnight and I've just come back from a dinner party where I was put down the end of the table with someone's respected grandmother and spinster aunt while all the fun stuff (between the couples) was happening at the other end of the room!

Grr ...

Esther

✉ Dear Esther

I am sorry you've been having an awful time of it. I don't think I will have all the answers to your questions. I know I am an elder's wife but it doesn't mean I have any wise solutions. But, I will do my best!

If you want to come round and have a chat please text me a time when you are free and you are welcome to pop in. I need sane conversation, as all I get here is football talk or 'What's for dinner?' I am also trying out some new recipes and I need an objective taster. However, I warn you the house may be full – at the moment the boys' friends have a knack of 'dropping in' just about the time I am doing my baking. Who tells them? Or do they just catch the waft of cupcakes on the wind and follow their noses?

As for getting jealous about laughter over the tea urn, there are times when the problem is an insecure wife, not a friendly single woman. Do not fret. Keep your heart right. What did you do wrong?

Don't let all the hassle you had at the mixer and at the dinner party upset you.

Wasn't it Augustine who said, 'The church is a whore but she's my mother'? Contrary to popular belief, the church can get it wrong. God doesn't.

Louise x

DATE: 25 OCTOBER

🖃 Hiya

I like that – St Augustine? Who'd have thought a fifth-century monk could be so intuitive and quite so honest?

By the way, did you know that he's also known as Augustine of Hippo?

Appropriate I think – when I came home after the terrible dinner I made my way through half a tub of cookie dough ice cream.

I've been trying to find something to be thankful for during these autumn days and I've found it.

Thank you Lord for ice cream. It has a way of helping, don't you think?

Esther x

DATE: 26 OCTOBER

✉ Hi Lou

Feeling loads better today. I've signed up two new contracts and I've been reading 2 Corinthians 12.

It is refreshing to read that Paul also had a 'thorn in his side'. Mine is singleness but I wonder what his was? Did I read somewhere that some people think it might have been a mother-in-law? I thought he was unmarried?

Anyway, one simple phrase in this reading captured me: 'My grace is sufficient for you'. Now, I know I'm probably taking it out of biblical context but those six little words really made me think. Why are we (why am I) constantly wittering on about the woes of singleness when actually I have everything I need? Why do I need a man? Surely I should be content 'just' with Jesus.

So, with that in mind I headed for the shops – specifically a hardware store – to get some plug un-blocker. The drains in my road are monstrous at the moment. My bathroom sink is constantly gurgling and overflowing. It's time to sort it out. I know what you would have said if I'd asked for an opinion: 'Call Sam!' but I was having one of those 'I'm a capable woman and I don't need a man to help me' moments.

As chance would have it, though, I bumped into Sam at the hardware store. He was exiting with an armful of pipes but very kindly came back into the shop and helped me select the carton of un-blocker. I keep forgetting, in all my self-pity, what a nice man he is.

Not only a taxi driver but also a knight in shining armour – well in overalls anyway!

E

PS I'm still dreaming about those NY hot dogs!

PPS How's Ollie? Still pining for the backstabbing Chloe?

DATE: 27 OCTOBER

✉ Hi Esther

This is a stay-at-home late half-term for us. We really can't afford to go away. Ollie is determined to win Chloe back from the lascivious Lewis. He's blaming Jack and me, of course, for forcing him to go on our Franch holiday and causing the subsequent loss of the love of his life!

Lou

PS Did I tell you that when I got back from NY it was to the news that Bobby fancies a girl in his class? Apparently the lovely Megs from France didn't last long. Despite the long goodbye, which we witnessed when she left the campsite, he's moved on. Such is life when you're fickle and 15.

He won't tell us her name but Laurence says she's called Mirabelle. It's Catherine and James' oldest. They start FAR too young these days.

📧 Hi Lou

I saw James the other day – he looks really sad. I felt really uncomfortable. When I asked him how the girls were he said they were doing well, although finding the to-ing and fro-ing between Catherine's place and his difficult. His little flat is on Cullan Avenue. He says it's a bit noisy, given that it's a main road, but it'll do for now. He didn't mention that Mirabelle had a beau – perhaps she hasn't told the parents yet?

E

✉ Hi Esther

Apparently Bobby and 'Bella' have held hands on the way home from school – which I think for Laurence is tantamount to an engagement! Bobby still insists she's 'just a good friend' but he has asked if she can come round for Sunday dinner one weekend.

They do grow up TOO quickly.

L xx

17

SUBJECT: TIMES THEY ARE A-CHANGING

DATE: 31 OCTOBER

Hi Lou

So, this Halloween I'm hoping NOT to be the victim of the ghastly trick or treaters.

I really don't understand this day. When on earth did our kids, and our nation, take on this bizarre 'festival'? Probably since it all became so commercialized. I'm not sure what I really think about it – satanic influences or harmless fun?

Perhaps it's because I'm English (well, half English anyway) but I just don't get it. I know some of our American friends embrace this sort of thing and think it's all very jolly – carved pumpkins and happy children in funny clothes. But I can't help thinking that its adoption on this side of the pond has more to do with the sales of sweets, candies, dressing-up outfits and vampire teeth! It's all so un-British – kids roaming the streets dressed as hobgoblins and witches, demanding sweets and screaming off down the avenue smacks of antisocial behaviour to me.

Last year Tom took me out for the evening, so I avoided the annual ritual of trying to ignore the kids when they knocked on the door, then hearing the eggs being thrown at the windows in disgust.

Tonight, I'm not even in the lounge. In previous years those tricky children and teenagers could see my light and knew I was in. Right now, I'm upstairs in the back bedroom, curtains closed and only the bedside light on.

OK. I admit it. I'm hiding from little children. It's confirmed. I'm a VERY SAD PERSON! Just thought I'd say.

Esther

 Hi E – come round to ours – we're just about to go out to a 'Light' party at church. Come join us. Not a witch or goblin in sight! L

DATE: 2 NOVEMBER

📄 Dear Lou

You and Jack are life-savers. The party was excellent. Thanks. Sorry haven't emailed before – it's all been a bit busy.

E

✉ Dear Esther

We did have fun, didn't we?

SO glad you enjoyed it. We haven't done a 'Light' party before – don't know why really. Being the Hope & Light Church it's sort of obvious but this was the first year anyone thought of it. Anyway, I thought it was excellent and definitely a great alternative to Halloween. I think it might become a tradition!

Haven't played all those silly games for years. Musical chairs – what a blast from the past!

I know you'll think it was contrived, but I honestly didn't realize Sam would be there. Was it a coincidence that you ended up sitting on his knee?

L

✉ Hi Lou

Saying nothing. Still blushing! Anyway, better Sam's knee than Ron's.
Did you see Sue's face when she realized that I was the only girl left
when there were three of us in the musical chairs final?

Is the honeymoon over already? That is the question.

E

DATE: 3 NOVEMBER

✉ Dear Esther

I saw Sue coming out of the doctors the other day. She told me she had
thought she was expecting but it was a false pregnancy. I must have that
kind of face. People are always telling me their most intimate details.

It does explain though why she was ultra-sensitive at the party the
other night. She has had a lot on her mind.

Anyway the doctor was happy for me, as I am happily
receiving therapy and it's working! He also said I was young –
to be on HRT. But the most important thing is . . . he said I was
young!

Lou

✉ Dear Louise

Actually Sue told me a couple of Sundays ago that she may have
some exciting news. I'll tread carefully next time I see her.

More importantly, I've also got some news for you. Before you ask,
NO Sam and I are NOT an item!

You know I travelled over to Naomi and Ken's yesterday – they
had some important news to relay, so I picked Mum up on the way. I
just assumed they, too, were expecting again – everywhere I look at
the moment there are pregnant women glowing!

But no, it's even more life changing than that.

Ken has always said that if the right job came up back home in Canada, they would consider relocating. Well, a job HAS come up and they ARE moving!

The most astonishing thing is that they are actually heading off later this month! Lots of issues to sort out, so a busy few weeks, but the bottom line is, it now looks like I'll be spending Christmas in Canada!

Still taking it all in.

Esther

✉ Dear Esther

I can't believe it – that's quick. What's the new job? Hasn't Ken got to give notice? What are they going to do with their house? Where are they going to live? Can you move THAT quickly to the other side of the world? Last time Jack and I moved it took us three years to decide on a new house and about a year to pack and unpack. I know Naomi is organized, but that's mad. And with two little boys!

She's going to need a lot of help and support. And so are you – I'm here if you need to chat.

Louise

🗐 Dear Lou

Thanks. I'm also still in shock. I'll miss them. Although we don't live in each other's pockets, I know they and Mum are always there. But it's a fantastic job offer and one that Ken just can't turn down!'

Answering some of the questions – I asked all these and more and Naomi and Ken had already worked it all out.

New job – head of the marketing dept at his (Ken's) old alma mater.

Old job – Ken only had to give one month's notice. With the holidays he is still due he can leave in a fortnight. He did query the one-month notice period when he got the job, and suggested three, but they didn't take it up. His new boss wants him there before Christmas to ease him into the role, which he takes up full-time in January!

Old house – will be rented after Christmas and then at some point when prices stabilize a bit they may sell. Meanwhile it'll be a little earner for them.

New house – they're returning to Quebec and will live in one of Ken's family's homes. You know he comes from a big family and they aren't short of a cent or two, so his parents have suggested they move into one of their 'cottages'. Naomi showed me a picture and it's huge. They may buy over there eventually but I think once they settle down in that big old house, they'll stay put for a while and just pay rent to Ken's mom and dad.

Yes, they CAN move that quickly. When I arrived at their house, the boxes in the hallway and the lack of pictures on the wall should have given me a clue as to their BIG NEWS but I just thought, 'Typical Naomi . . . another clear-out!'

I'm actually going over tomorrow to help with the packing. It is going to be a bit of a rush but Naomi has it all in hand. The fact that she's not a hoarder, unlike me, means that she lives in a pretty organized state anyway.

Did I tell you that when we were kids she used to make money on the side tidying other kids' rooms? She had 'business cards' and a business plan. It went like this. A kid who had a trashed room and was getting it in the neck from the parents would invite Naomi round for a 'play date' or a 'study date' and then she'd tidy their room for them. She was a right little junior entrepreneur.

The removals people are already booked and the stuff will be 'containered' and shipped shortly. If it had been me, I would have ensured everything arrived after Christmas but Naomi wants it with them asap. So, undoubtedly, my Christmas holidays will be spent helping to unpack! As Ken's new workplace (the university) is paying for it all, it's all being fast tracked, at great expense.

As for the boys, Kenny Jr and Kai are going with the flow and are looking forward to being with their Canadian gramps and granny, and all their aunts, uncles and cousins. It's probably a good age for them to move – not really established in education here – but I'm still going to miss them like crazy.

E

PS Forgot to ask – do you have any packing boxes you don't need? I thought you once said you had some in your garage from the last time you moved. If so, can Naomi borrow them please?

DATE: 4 NOVEMBER

 Esther

Tell Naomi that of course she can have the packing boxes – they've been sitting flattened in our garage for a few years and, after the trauma of our last move, I'm not going to be needing them anytime soon. I'm guessing from this that she had more stuff to pack than she thought?

L

 Ta Lou, I'll drive back over from Naomi's this p.m. to pick up boxes. Naomi sends love.

DATE: 6 NOVEMBER

 Dear Louise

I know you'll pick this up tomorrow morning (actually it'll be this morning . . . didn't realize it was this late . . .) when you log on, but just back from Naomi's and needed to fill you in on some MORE earth-shattering news!

As you know, Mum was also helping with the packing and, when I got back with your flat boxes (thanks by the way!), it was obvious that she and Naomi had been chatting.

The upshot is – Mum has decided that she is also going to return to Canada! I know she's been hankering after spending more time there but the move of her only grandchildren to the other side of the Atlantic has decided her. Of course, she didn't tell me outright but instead asked, 'What would you think if . . . ?' And, of course, I couldn't say, 'DON'T GO!!' . . . It all makes perfect sense doesn't it?

But . . . It's a lot to take in.

E ☹

✉ Dear E

Actually Jack and I are still up – we were waiting for the boys to get back from the Bonfire Night party on the lower field at school. They've ambled in smelling of woodsmoke and hotdogs and Laurence tells me he now thinks he might like to be a 'pyrotechnician' when he 'grows up'. Last week he wanted to be a racing driver and a couple of months ago we had a budding vet on our hands. Who knows where he'll end up but Jack and I are hoping the firework phase wears off pretty quickly. Meanwhile, we decided against the roar of the fire and the smell of the gunpowder and opted for a rare quiet night in – just the two of us – and it's been sheer bliss.

I'm shocked to hear your mum has also decided to leave the UK. You must feel terrible. Tell you what, I'll skip Bible class and come round – how's that?

Louise xxx

 Thanks SO much, Lou! Yes, please come. Will be good to talk, try to get it all straight in my head, and maybe weep just a little. E xx

 Waterproofing my shoulder and digging out the tissues. Will bring cake. Lou x

 Thanks. E xx

18

SUBJECT: LAST-MINUTE STRESSING AND PACKING

DATE: 28 NOVEMBER

✉ Dear Esther

It seems ages since we chatted properly!

Did everyone get away OK? Did they all arrive safely? How did Kai and Kenny Jr cope with the flight? Come to that, how did your mum and the adults cope with the flight, with two such excited little boys?

Hope you're still coming round for Sunday lunch, as planned.

Did I tell you I popped in to Wendleworth's the other day? Still trying to avoid the boy manager and it wasn't long before I saw him standing with a clipboard next to the cold meats section. I ducked down behind a large display of baked beans, and I was mesmerized. I could only see him from the side, but there was something different about him, and I couldn't quite work out what it was.

I turned around and bumped into POG, and then I twigged – all these men seem to have sprouted facial hair. It took me a moment to realize that there's a bunch of wonderful men in our town growing beards and moustaches for 'Movember'. And Simon had a little moustache. You could hardly see it he's so fair, but it was a very good attempt. It did, in fact, make him look slightly older. Which has to be good when you are in charge of a large team in a substantially sized supermarket. Looking like someone who is just dropping in for a few bits and pieces for your mum on your way home from school must be a handicap when you are trying to exert some authority over underlings.

It's been a while now since the Fairtrade Easter egg incident and I do feel it's time to bury the hatchet. Not literally, of course. So, in the spirit of reconciliation, I breathed deeply, emerged from behind the beans and approached Simon. When he heard me say his name he raised his head and for a moment he looked like a little (moustached) rabbit in a headlight. I could see what was going through his mind: 'Oh no . . . not her . . . can't escape, at least not without charging into an enormous stack of beans that took two of my staff several hours to create!'

You would have been proud of me. I was very polite. I apologized for 'all that misunderstanding over the Fairtrade chocolate' and thanked him for his impressive stocks of the stuff. That's a result, don't you think?

Simon seemed to relax and looked less ready to run for the hills. I then mentioned that it was very good to see that he was participating in 'Movember' and offered to give him a £20 donation.

He thanked me. I think I even saw him smile. We might have an understanding now, which means maybe I can start shopping in Wendleworth's without having to dress in disguise or wear a moustache myself!

I love the idea of 'Movember' – being the mother of boys I do worry about their health and am constantly nagging them to 'look after themselves'. But, as we know, men don't really pay as much attention to this as us women. I have no idea who came up with the idea of getting men to grow facial hair to raise awareness of men's health issues but he/she is BRILLIANT! Raises money for great charities and gets people talking about stuff they'd rather not address. Has to be good.

Jack has never grown a beard. Maybe I will challenge him to do so next year. It would also be a great way to start a conversation with all my boys about the need to be alert to bumps and lumps that might appear on bits of their body that they think I don't know about. That conversation can't be any more embarrassing than the 'serious sex talk' Jack and I had to have with Ollie, Bobby and Laurence earlier this year. Can it?

L xx

✉ Hi Louise

Not sure I'll have a chance to pop into the shop to have a look at the boy manager's attempt at facial hair, at least not before Movember is out. Pity. I would have liked to see that. But if Jack decides to participate next year, I'll be sure to sponsor him. It would be worth the money to see him with a hairy upper lip and coping with the whole rather unkempt look.

Sorry, I'd completely forgotten about Sunday lunch. Do you mind if I dip out? I don't really quite feel up to a big meal with family, even with your lovely crowd. Hope you'll understand. These last three weeks have been mad. What with my workload exploding in the run up to Christmas and all the family business I don't feel I've had time to breathe.

We only finished packing up Mum's flat three days ago and I'm going to handle the shipping and the sale in the New Year. There was a very tearful goodbye at the airport – even though I'm going to see them all in three weeks it all felt so permanent.

They've arrived safely to a huge family reunion. I saw the pictures on Facebook!

Mum is going to live with Naomi and Ken for a bit, while she looks for a new place. She thinks that a community for retired folk would be best for her. 'It's not an old people's home!' she insists, but thinks it's the best option. I tend to agree. There are a few really excellent retirement communities in the area where Ken and Naomi are settling. And as she originally comes from that part of the world her sisters and nephews/nieces are all in the general area and none more than an hour's drive away. So she will be near family members.

All family members ... except me, of course.

Must go – I need to write a report for a client that's due tomorrow. I've been putting it off but deadline is looming.

Esther

DATE: 29 NOVEMBER

✉ Dear Esther

Understand totally about Sunday lunch. Being surrounded by 'happy family' may not be that helpful for you right now. I can't believe that it's my family I'm talking about, but, on reflection, we ARE a happy family – even though my husband seems to be away more than at home at the moment, my finances are spiralling out of control, our eldest son still blames us for his broken heart and our youngest son has now also fallen in love – with 'Mary', a rather large dog he met in the local pound. He is determined that he will have nagged us into adopting her by Christmas.

But please don't hide away for too long! Please do not sit alone and lonely.

I could bring round a plate – my version of meals on wheels? Please look after yourself!

Love

Louise

🖅 Dear Lou

Thanks for the food offer. Will be very happy to receive anything in the way of provisions – it was only when I read your message that I looked in my fridge and realized that its sole contents were one egg, a little milk and half an onion. I need to get to the shops.

I've spent so much time at Naomi's and Mum's recently that I've not been home to eat or cook. I was going to have an omelette tonight, and I hadn't thought as far ahead as Sunday.

Thanks SO much. Report nearly done.

E

Going food shopping this evening. Want to come? Not very glamorous but will get you away from the computer. L xx

Date: 4 December

✉ Hi Esther

Only a fortnight now to your holiday! Have you started packing yet? Have you got everything you need for your trip?

Just to keep you in the loop – Laurence HAS worn us down and Jack and I have agreed that Mary can come live with us so long as she has her bed in the utility room and is not allowed upstairs. It'll be nice to have another female in the house, even if she is hairy and rather smelly!

Laurence has PROMISED that he'll walk her – wonder how long that will last? Meanwhile I'm thinking that a few walks with a dog may be good for my weight. Still determined to lose a few more pounds before the Christmas glutton fest gets underway. Every year I promise myself that we won't indulge excessively and I really do think we have cut down on the unnecessary food consumption in the past few years. But we always get so many 'treats' given to us – my clients, Jack's clients, church friends and more – that are hard to resist.

Saw Sam at church and didn't give away the fact that I knew he took you to the cinema the other night. I know I'm being nosey, but how did it go? What did you see? At least it must take your mind off your mum and the rest of the family.

Lou x

Dear Lou

Not as organized as I need to be for the trip to Canada. Life has been so hectic. Lots of PR work in the run up to Christmas – everyone wants their message out. It's good but it doesn't leave much time for anything else and normally I'm not needing to organize an international flight and other stuff too!

First, how many pairs of trousers do you think I need for this holiday? Now wishing I had updated the wardrobe a bit. Maybe have to go shopping in Canada. Just hope I don't lose all my new stuff – still grieving a little over all my lost New York shopping. Because I got some compensation from the hotel I decided not to claim insurance but I will secretly miss my 'I Love Jesus' bag when I fly next week.

As for Sam – we had a very nice evening. The film was great and we went for a pizza afterwards. I'm still not sure whether I want to jump into another relationship, but I am aware that I've left him hanging on a string for a while now and he is very keen, I know.

I'm thinking that maybe THAT was my problem with Tom – I kept him hanging around too long, before making a commitment, and then, within months of becoming 'officially engaged' and when all the wedding palaver took over life, he stood back and thought, 'Do I want this? Forever?' Once he had me, he realized he didn't want me! I know you've said that it was nothing I did, and even though I am putting it all in the past, I do occasionally lie awake at night wondering if I could have done things differently, not kept him waiting around, etc.

Anyway, I have been feeling a bit guilty about not spending much time with Sam recently – well apart from that day when I had to get him round to Mum's flat to sort out that broken pipe . . . thank goodness it happened before we closed up the place for the winter – so I did say sorry.

He was very sweet. 'No need to apologize. Not as if we're serious.' But his expression told me what he really wanted to say was, 'WHEN are we going to get serious?'

And, to add to my confusion, I received an email from Tom this morning, which is a bit weird to say the least.

I need to have a good long think about all this. Perhaps being away in Canada might help after all. Am glad I'm going. It'll take my mind off the whole 'almost a year since Tom and I split up' thing.

E x

PS Forwarding Tom's email.

From: Tom.e.fellows@fellowsmail.com

Dear Esther

I am finding this a hard email to write. I wanted to see you again before you emigrated but it sounds like we can't do that. I cannot believe that you are going to Canada. I know we have not seen each other for a while but I always thought I knew where you would be. In my mind you were in the same house, doing the same job. You were always there.

You know how hard it is for me to express my feelings and to talk about the past, but I am beginning to realize now that most of the time we were together was amazing and I am so thankful for the years we had. Maybe it is because it's Christmas time again and the approach of a New Year — I am not sure — but I do know I still have feelings for you. In my heart I am beginning to wonder if we should try again.

I have been thinking a lot about us and so has Mum. She will probably be in contact again as well. I know how much you respect her so I hope you won't mind her being in touch. In fact, it was Mum who told me that the whole family was returning to Canada — you know she's been meeting up with your mum since we split up?

I know Mum hears from God and she still feels we should be together. It's been a long time since I thought about God and, in fact, it was our difference in spirituality that made me leave. You were so determined to put God first and I just couldn't handle that — I realize that, despite this fundamental difference, she may be right.

Life hasn't been the same since we split up. I've sort of ambled along since we finished last January and I can't seem to get my act together at all. None of the relationships I've had have worked out and I realize now that you may be, after all, the woman for me.

Please think about this. How do you feel about me? Don't waste the years we spent together. Reconsider and phone me if you get a chance.

Love

Tom

DATE: 6 DECEMBER

✉ Esther

Reconsider what? Don't you dare reconsider Tom! Remember the pain of those first few months? Esther you were a wreck. I cannot let you do this again!

Do not let him wriggle back into your life just when things are changing.

And what about Sam? You say you're 'just friends' but surely it is more? Has all that plumbing been to no avail?

Louise x

DATE: 7 DECEMBER

🖅 Dear Lou

Hope you're sitting down – don't be too shocked or upset.

I've decided to meet up with Tom tomorrow night. I feel I need to talk to him. I want him to know the truth – he's obviously got majorly confused about my situation. Mum obviously mentioned to Harriet that she was moving back to Canada with 'the family' (i.e. Naomi and Ken and the boys) and Tom's mum jumped to the conclusion that 'the family' also included me. He's panicked and thinks he's lost me forever.

And, of course, the real truth is . . . he has!

Don't worry. I'm not going to take him back. I lost the Tom I thought I knew when he told me he didn't love me just after New Year. My heart broke when he told me he didn't want me or the wedding – along with the dress, cake and fab wedding venue! He didn't want our planned future and couldn't see us growing old together. I know I'm an old romantic but I'm a girl, and I had it all mapped out for us.

When he made his pronouncement and left, I discovered that he was, in fact, a rather cold, heartless man who just walked away from what I thought was a great friendship, relationship and future.

As you see from his email, he's blaming our 'difference in spirituality' for his change of heart, but, as you know, that wasn't the entire story. Yes, he was always jealous of the time I spent in church and with my Christian friends, especially you. I can tell you that now. He often moaned about the fun and laughter we enjoyed; he was so possessive and he resented it. Bit of a power freak, truth be told. He was even jealous of the time I spent at work and, as you know, in that last year with him I did neglect my business a little, what with the wedding plans and the fact that I could never take on contracts that involved trips away because he didn't like it.

But I do think that wasn't all. There was another major reason that he walked. One time, towards the end when he was being cruel (looking back I realize there were signs that the relationship was in danger but I didn't want to admit it to myself), he threw my age in my face. We were chatting about the future and I said I'd really like to start trying for a baby as soon as we were married (I needed to know he was OK with that). He just laughed and said something like, 'That's fine, darling, but don't get your hopes up . . . you are a bit old to have kids, I think you know that!'

I know you warned me when Tom and I got together that hooking up with a man nine years my junior might not be the best option, but I was swept off my feet. I'd never felt so desirable before. I'd spent so many years feeling slightly unattractive – not sure why because I realize now that I wasn't any worse looking than most 'ordinary' women. OK, not God's gift to the world, but certainly not a female Quasimodo! Then along came this sexy, gorgeous young man who paid attention to me, lavished gifts on me and wanted me.

We've had this conversation before, I know, but I repeat – why is it that men can date/marry/be with women decades their junior and no one bats an eyelid, but when a woman gets together with a younger man it seems society frowns?

I ignored the snide comments and the nastiness but I always guessed that Tom found that hard to cope with. I'm absolutely sure now that my age had something to do with his decision to break our engagement. He couldn't stand the 'What's the gorgeous man doing with that old woman?' side glances!

Anyway, for me that is all now well and truly in the past. Although I know Tom will always hold a place somewhere in the corner of my heart, I can't trust him. In fact I don't think I even want him as a friend. My broken heart is still mending.

Did you see what he wrote? 'Life hasn't been the same since we split up . . . can't get my act together . . . none of the relationships I've had have worked out . . . realize now that you may after all be the woman for me.'

That just made me mad. I guessed he'd had girlfriends but none of these obviously looked after him like I did: doing his washing, cooking for him – just like his mother, but more! Anyway, I'm going to tell him tomorrow, 'Goodbye and good luck!'

This is not a decision I have to pray and fast about. God has given me common sense for a reason.

Esther

✉ Dear Esther

You may not have to pray about it but I will pray for you tomorrow. Be strong. Don't let those big brown eyes do you in again. I was also furious to see what Tom wrote. Hope you don't mind but I showed Jack and he was also mad, mad, mad! And what he said was spot on: 'The man doesn't know what he wants. If Esther takes him back he'll dump her again first time another bit of skirt comes along.' I think Jack's right!

Also, although some think that whole 'don't be unequally yoked' with a non-Christian teaching has been rather overemphasized in church over the years I've begun to understand the deep truth in those words. Tom had a real problem with your faith and Jack and I were always privately worried that once you were married he might gradually pull you away from your Christian life. Being a Christian is such a huge part of who you are. If the one you are sharing your life with does not share that fundamental foundation and motivation with you, you are setting off on a difficult path. We've seen it happen before, even with people like you who have a strong faith.

I don't need to remind you that Tom's lack of Christian faith was the reason why you put off the 'full commitment' to engagement and marriage in the first place. Remember all those long conversations (and emails) about your dilemma over several years?

Anyway, as I said before. Be strong! Let me know how it goes.

Love and prayers

Louise

PS Jack says he can take you to the airport this week if you want. Jacqui and I will be busy with that big Christmas cupcake order for the hospital – thank goodness for some work. But Jack can make himself available as taxi driver.

PPS Did Tom REALLY love you for your cooking?!

✉ Dear Lou

Actually Sam said he will give me a lift to the airport so thank Jack for me and tell him I am sorted ta. Will keep you posted on the Tom thing.

Esther

PS Tom and I did go out to eat a lot.

DATE: 9 DECEMBER

✉ Dear Lou

Update.

I saw Sam for coffee yesterday morning and, although as you say we're 'just friends' at the moment, I felt I should tell him about my upcoming 'date' with Tom. You know this town – news gets round so quickly and I didn't want him to hear it from anyone else.

He looked a little pale, but when I explained that I didn't intend to get back together with my 'ex' his colour improved. In fact, he did something quite amazing. He leaned over and picked up my hand and asked me if he could pray for me. And right there, in The Crooked Teapot, he said a little prayer for me. Can't tell you what he prayed for, my heart was beating so fast, not just because he was holding my hand but also because I was overwhelmed with his generosity and compassion.

It was just what I needed to help me to gird my loins for the meeting with Tom, in the new tapas restaurant on the High Street. I've been wanting to try it out, so I thought it was a good moment. Neutral territory! No past memories associated with it. I was also very pleased that I'd told Sam because the first people we saw in the place were Allegra and Jason – and you know what a huge gossip HE is!

I have to admit, Tom still looked good. Not quite as together as when he came round for the books a few months back when I was still yearning for him, but still good. I had to keep reminding myself of what he did in January. He apologized for all the hurt. I was trying really hard not to flare up. I think I read the menu six times at least and the poor old waiter lurked in anticipation for what must have seemed like years before we eventually ordered.

Tom begged me not to go to Canada and I didn't even get a chance to tell him I wasn't emigrating. He started whining that we should get back together, that we were made for each other. He couldn't go on without me. His mother has refused to do his laundry and only Harriet and I knew how to starch his shirts in the way he liked them. He wanted me back, he wanted to marry me (again) and said: 'Even if you can't have babies because you're so old, I don't mind any more! I don't need offspring. Maybe we could adopt?' The final barb, however, was, 'And anyway, Esther, let's face it, you'll not get anyone else, not at your age so we may as well get back together'!

Once I managed to get a word in I told him I couldn't really see that a life spent starching his shirts, not having his babies and putting up with his vanity and his jealously of my faith and my friends would be any good at all . . . for me! I thanked him for the good times (and I meant it) and then said that even though I didn't know what God had in store for me or whether it involved me being happily married, I knew one thing. My future didn't include him.

Then I walked out, just as the waiter was bringing a rather expensive platter to the table. Sorry, I still can't tell you if the tapas is any good.

I was shaking when I left the building and, as I knew you were unavailable (by the way, hope the slimming club went well again), I went to see Sam. After the hand-holding moment in The Crooked Teapot he'd hinted that I could pop round to his if I needed to and he'd be there with tissues and tea.

He was true to his word. He let me blub and curl up and watch TV for a while. He didn't even ask me how I got on. He didn't need to. There was no cuddling – well, not much . . .

So Tom has gone – for good. I'm glad it's all sorted in my head before Canada. I will call in tomorrow after church.

One sad but at peace E x

19

SUBJECT: NEWS FROM A FAR COUNTRY

Date: 19 December

Hi E, are you OK? Heard what happened at the airport. Hope the journey wasn't too traumatic as a result! Email when you land – please. Love L

Dear Lou

Am here safely and no trauma!

Well not more than the usual economy class hell on a busy pre-Christmas flight. The man in front of me (rather too large and heavy for a rather small seat) decided to remain reclined for most of the flight, which left me rather squashed – in fact he may as well have been sitting on my lap! I was nearly garrotted by my fold-down table at meal times.

Also, in my part of the cabin there was an awful toddler whose mother obviously does not know the meaning of discipline. His screams could have broken glass. Everyone just pulled on their headphones and turned the volume up. Actually, after a few hours of this, I began to feel quite sorry for the mummy. Imagine having to live with that hour in hour out, day in day out, week in week out? What a nightmare.

I had a nice text from Sam when I arrived. He was on his way to the new members' class Christmas 'do'.

So – the airport. You heard? Due to heavy traffic en route, I was nearly late to check in. Sam dropped me at the door and then went to park and I rushed to the desk.

I checked my bags and Sam ran in and we made our way to the departures gate. Imagine my horror when I saw Tom there! How he knew what flight I was on I have no idea.

Frosty would not describe Tom's reaction to Sam. He basically ignored him, grabbed me and started begging me to stay. I just wanted to shout, 'I am a new me! I don't want you! You don't own me!' but I wanted to avoid screaming in public, so I just struggled clear of his embrace muttering, 'No Tom!' Undeterred, he followed us towards passport control and the departure gates.

Poor Sam wasn't sure what to do. At first, I wondered if he thought I had invited Tom to the airport. So, throwing caution to the wind, I stopped walking and, in a very loud voice (you would have been proud), said quite clearly, 'Please go away Tom! We're finished! I told you that the other day!'

At this point, Tom grabbed hold of me again and, right there near the departure gates in front of all the security staff and hundreds of inquisitive passengers, got on his knees and pleaded with me not to leave him. He literally had his arms round my feet. It was so embarrassing. The whole airport seemed to stop around us, everything went quiet and there must have been 500 people or more looking at me.

At this point Sam had had enough. He addressed the prostrate Tom, quite quietly but firmly, and said something like, 'I think you need to go now mate.' I was trying to make my way through the gates to passport control but that resulted in me pulling my ex-fiancé along the shiny floor. From my left I could see security guards approaching.

It would be fair to say I can't clearly remember what happened next. Sam, I think, lifted Tom by the collar and forced him to his feet. Tom swung for him and punched him in the face. Sam, who I had no idea was so macho, did a sort of defensive manoeuvre and tackled Tom to the floor. I was shaken, Tom was stunned, and some people nearby started clapping! One of the security guards asked me if I needed assistance. I explained that Tom was harassing me and that Sam had come to my rescue. I think there was an offer of the first aid room for Sam, which was declined. The security men then decided they needed to 'escort this gentleman from the building'.

How I said goodbye to Sam, got through security and onto the plane I am unsure. I was still shaking halfway across the Atlantic. It's at times like this that I wish I drank. I would have had a whisky, or five, and been out like a light, and neither the airport incident nor the big man in front would have bothered me.

But I've arrived safely, and no hangover! It's night here and I'm exhausted.

Speak soon

Esther x

DATE: 20 DECEMBER

✉ Dear Esther

Thank you for filling me in. Actually Sam came round and told us that there had been an 'incident' but we didn't get all the details, apart from the bit about Tom being dragged across the floor and the punching moments! Sam was really worried about the effect it had had on you but Jack and I ended up seeing how funny it must have looked to the spectators and had a good laugh. Hope you don't mind?

Have a great holiday and a wonderful Christmas! I will miss catching up properly but will aim to inform you of any newsworthy reports over the next few weeks – gossip, I know. Isn't it amazing? You did take your iPad didn't you? While you're over there perhaps we can chat via FaceTime from time to time?

Hopefully it will be a slimmer me that meets you at the airport. I have found a great outfit for New Year and want to wear it. I think you will like it. I got it yesterday. Amazing how so many of the stores now start their post-Christmas sales before the festive season!

Meanwhile, Jack is on the lookout for Tom – to beat him up in a loving Christian way! Anyway, à bientôt to Esther in French Canada.

Louise

Date: 22 December

✉ Dear Esther

I can't believe that Geoff is marrying again. How long since Angela
departed? Maybe he is a man who just needs female company. There
are some men like that. You would think after being released from a
lifetime of domestic servitude he would delight in his freedom! But
no . . .

How did you find out?

And Sue is pregnant? How do you get all your information while
you are in Canada?!

Jack and I were joking that Sue may use the tie-dyed wedding
dress to make a christening gown. I wonder if the christening
party will be as mad as the wedding? I know you escaped but I
had lunch with Leggy Lynda the other day – part of the planning
for the joint churches' Christmas craft sale – and she filled me in
on the details.

Did you know that Sue and Ron's guests went home with Fairtrade
stickers for their cars as their favours? The bridesmaids were only
three- and four-years-old – they wore rainbow dungarees and carried
flags with signs of doves on them. The crème de la crème was the
bride. Lynda said that, like all brides, Sue did look beautiful, despite
her 'unusual' wedding attire. The wedding dress did look exquisite but
what was not so cool was the red silk banner she wore across her dress
with the words 'Happy birthday Ron' emblazoned on it. The wedding
cake also had birthday candles on it! We knew it was his birthday and
that's why the date was important to them, but really . . . And although
most of the music was 'traditional', the happy couple left the church to
the song 'Da Doo Ron Ron' (the choir singing the refrain and including
slightly altered words 'I do Ron Ron, I do Ron Ron').

Definitely not the sophisticated affair your wedding would have
been.

Louise

PS What's Naomi's new place like? Not seen anything on Facebook. Has your mum started looking for her new abode yet? Pictures please!

PPS Decided I am having a makeover. I am so fed up with myself just now. No one is noticing the weight loss!

DATE: 24 DECEMBER

📧 Hi Louise

Canada is wonderful. COLD but brilliant! I have just put some amazing photos on Facebook.

To answer all your questions in order …

Rev T 'Facebooked' me privately to tell me about POG. The most shocking news, though, is that he's not marrying Margaret but someone called Aggie. She's a librarian and is 35! He's a new man! Tired, I guess, but new. They'll be married sometime in the New Year. Await baby news I guess …Yikes!

On the preggers front, the Sue news came via Penny. She emailed me and said she'd been home for a visit and bumped into Sue in town, who is already sticking out her stomach and wearing voluminous tie-dyed maternity outfits even though she can't be more than six weeks gone! She asked to be remembered to me and wondered why she hadn't heard from me recently.

I'm still fuming with her. I showed you the Christmas card I had from her and Ron, didn't I? I knew I'd get a few 'To Tom and Esther' or 'To Esther and Tom' cards from people who hadn't heard that the big romance was over – I didn't get around to announcing it to the whole world and as this time last year we WERE still together, it's not their fault. But I couldn't believe I got a 'Happy Christmas Tom and Esther' card from Sue and Ron! Did they not remember that they took MY wedding day, and she had MY wedding dress? But I'm not going to get stressed again. I'm thousands of miles away and it's lovely here. As I said, very cold, but beautiful.

I always forget how amazing Quebec is and then I get here and am stunned all over again. Naomi and Ken have a beautiful home, large and rambling with a huge garden. You can't see much of the acre at the moment because the snow is up to our armpits. But it will be beautiful when they have made it 'home'. It's the house that Ken's grandparents – his 'mémé' and 'pépé' (isn't that sweet?) – lived in most of their married life. They're both gone now and it's been empty for a while, so it needs a little work doing on it. Ken's brother Matthew has already been round and they've started to make plans. It's an astonishing upgrade from the little town house that was all they could afford in England.

The day after I arrived we went to see a lovely apartment on the local retirement complex, which will be just perfect for Mum. Her furniture from home will look beautiful in it when it arrives. Two large bedrooms (I have been told one is for me for my many visits and for when I eventually come to my senses and also emigrate to join the family and need somewhere to stay while I search for my own place). Only a mile or so from Naomi's, it will be perfect for babysitting and for the boys to pop in because it's on the outskirts of town, so when they are old enough they will be able to walk up to Granny's from school.

The retirement complex has everything – a pool and a health spa/gym (Jack would like it!), tennis courts and other outdoor facilities for when it's not all under ten feet of snow. The people there seem really nice and they organize all kinds of social activities. I think Mum's coming round to the idea of 'communal living'. Plus it's not far from a really great church – lively and lots of young people as well as activities for 'seniors'. She is working on Naomi and Ken and I think has already persuaded them to send Kai and Kenny Jr to Sunday school. They haven't done much church stuff in recent years so we're praying this will be a good way back in for them.

By the way, the ski jacket has had an airing. I know you thought I was mad to take it but we all went snowboarding the other day and it was fantastic. I fell over – a lot – but we laughed so much. I can't remember the last time I've laughed like that. It's been a long time. We were joined by some of Ken's family and Kai and Kenny Junior were in their element with all their cousins. They'll soon be ski and snowboard experts. I'm going to miss seeing them grow up. We also went ice-skating and I fell over again. A lot. Matthew was very chivalrous and picked me up. A lot. He's round the house most days, helping Ken and Naomi to get things settled. Their container arrived a day or two after me and it was a rush to get it all sorted before Christmas but we managed it. Matthew is very capable. And I'd forgotten how dishy he is.

By the way, Colin needs to go round to my flat to pick up some papers on Tuesday. I've told him to pop by yours and get the keys. Is that OK?

Hope you're all fine there. Happy Christmas to you all!

Esther

20

SUBJECT: THE NEW YEAR

✉ Dear Esther

Happy Boxing Day!

Did you enjoy Christmas? Did you have turkey? . . . Sorry we didn't get a chance to FaceTime. Our day was just so busy, and what with the time difference . . .

Bet you were driven mad by your nephews again. What time did they wake you this year? I remember what it used to be like with our boys . . . this Christmas we had to wake them up in time for church, and pressies did not get ripped open until after lunch.

Jack loved his £200 trainers – sorry, running shoes. He reminded me that he isn't in 'training' for anything as he has decided against another half-marathon at the moment. I was glad he was pleased but all I could think of was the hundreds of cupcakes I had to bake to earn the money for those shoes.

I was presented with a 'swarp'. Until yesterday I had no idea there was such a thing. It is a mixture of a scarf and a wrap and it's beautiful, soft, woollen and tartan – actually in my Scottish granny's tartan, which would have pleased her no end if she was still around.

This swarp sort of wraps around you and is clipped with a pewter brooch. It really is lovely. Very impressed with Jack but then he does buy good presents. So I wore it to church on Christmas day morning. Someone told Jack they liked my blanket!

From a lovely warm and cosy Lou . . . the perfect example of a fashionable mummy.

☐ Hi Louise

Had a great fun Christmas! This year Santa's call came at 3.30 a.m. – a slight improvement on last year's unearthly 2.25! The boys are growing up.

The moon was still high and we sat in the moonlit lounge with the curtains wide open unwrapping Father Christmas presents. Ken fell back to sleep quite quickly and was snoring for Canada when we all returned to bed about 4.15 a.m. We left him there, covered up with OUR granny's crocheted blanket and a little note saying, 'When you wake up – start breakfast!' And he did – bless him!

We were treated to scrambled egg and salmon with fresh orange juice. It was a lovely start to a lovely day. It did feel strange not going to church on Christmas morning but, in the hours between leaving Ken on the couch and breakfast, we'd had one almighty blizzard and there was no shifting the car, even though it's a 4 x 4.

Uncle Matthew came by mid-morning, having managed to get through the drifts in his tank of a vehicle. He managed to get us all to Ken's mom and dad's house for Christmas Day festivities. With all the family (the ones who could make it anyway) we were fifteen for lunch. Noisy and rather crazy. People screaming in English and French Canadian. My ear is very quickly tuning in again but I did miss a lot of the family jokes.

No turkey but a brilliant goose. And no Brussels sprouts. Very happy. However, Naomi had packed a couple of large Christmas puddings in her luggage. We managed to find them in time for the big day and the reaction from the Canadians was mixed. Some loved the 'plum pudding', while others thought it was 'different'. The younger ones, in particular, announced it to be 'disgusting'. Matt loved it and winked at me over the Christmas table saying stuff like 'lovely ENGLISH grub' in a sort of fake British accent. Cute.

But having missed church on Christmas morning (I thought of you all crammed into Hope & Light with the Rivers of Life crowd) I am glad I spent time during the Advent period to think about what Christmas is all about. No matter how hard we try, we are impacted by all the consumerism and, although I attempt not to get too caught up in the 'Buy, Buy, Buy' craziness that comes with the month of December in the UK, I do sometimes not quite manage to be good. Having said that, I absolutely loved seeing the happiness in Kai and Kenny Jr's face when they opened my pressies to them. That idea you had – the British football kits – was inspired. Got to try to keep them a little 'British', eh?

How was your three-bird roast?

Are you still up for the sales when I get back?

Can you still pick me up from the airport even though it's New Year's Eve?

Sorry you're not coming to the New Year's Eve do at church . . . but I'll be there . . . with the time difference I'll still be awake at dawn! But I am so glad it's not another terrible New Year fancy dress affair. Mum still laughs about the photos I sent her showing me in my Pocahontas outfit.

E

DATE: 27 DECEMBER

✉ Hi Esther

I still laugh about that night! When they invited us and they told us it was an 'Indian New Year' celebration how were we to know they meant Asian not (Native) American? I still remember the look on everyone's faces when we turned up – them in their saris and dhotis (I think that's what the men were wearing) – us in our American Indian feathers and Jack with a full 'war bonnet' and war paint! We were so lucky no one was offended but I doubt we will ever get a job in the diplomatic service.

Sorry, changed my mind about shopping – I don't think I can cope with any more right now. The days running up to Christmas were completely mad.

The day you flew out to Canada, I went into Wendleworth's to try to pick up a few bits and pieces for the Christmas shopping. Since making my peace with the boy manager over the Fairtrade egg situation, I now feel confident once again to step over the threshold.

The shop was heaving. Two women were actually arguing over the last pair of men's socks on display. And the socks were hideous – bright red with what looked like Father Christmases on them – can't imagine my Jack wearing those.

There was another woman who had so much food in her trolley that it overturned mid-aisle. Does ANYONE need THREE turkeys? It conjured up images of her on a mountainside with five thousand souls waiting for lunch. Judging from the vast quantities in her basket she wouldn't even have needed Jesus on site to help feed them all!

We were still a week away from Christmas at this point. If I took all that food home that early – chocolates, puddings, sweets, nuts, raisins – it would have all been scoffed well ahead of the big day.

As it was, our three-bird roast turned out to be a two-bird. Our new family member, the delightful and ever hungry Mary, decided to make a meal of the chicken early on Christmas morning. How she managed to get to it I'll never know. It was defrosting out of harm's way on the work surface, and she, theoretically, was in the utility room. Fortunately it must have defrosted by the time she got to it, as she wasn't ill!

Up to then, Mary had only indulged in a passion for socks. She's eaten her way through most of Jack's socks. She doesn't touch mine, or the boys' socks. Just Jack's. Maybe I should have fought over the hideous Father Christmas socks after all.

But Wendleworth's was just too much. I ended up with a bit of a panic attack, which wasn't eased by an incident I witnessed involving my new 'mate' Simon. I rounded the corner of an aisle and there he was, with his clipboard, being harangued by some mad middle-aged woman who was ranting on about the 'lack of Fairtrade chocolates in your Christmas display! You had Fairtrade EASTER eggs but nothing, nothing at Christmas!'

Remind you of anyone? Simon didn't even notice me – I guess his chocolate affections have moved on.

After that experience, I turned to the internet to try a little pre-Christmas purchasing. I've not done this much before but it was great. I got Jack's new trainers (sorry, running shoes) and also some things for the boys. While online, I also discovered some great undies in the M&S New Year sale, which has already started and will probably be on 'til Easter. Very pleased because all the shopping arrived within two days.

Oh, and I also found a lovely hot pink cable cardigan with fluffy lining on another site. I like it but it did not go down well in all quarters. I was modelling my purchase for Jack (not the underwear) when the boys came into the room and told me I looked like a cupcake. I was not amused!

Right now, I have just about had enough of mopping up snotty tissues and all manner of debris that three teenagers and a husband leave at their elbows when suffering from Christmas flu. I have now also surrendered to the bug so 22 Arkland Street is a contagion zone.

I was meant to be making some little cupcakes today with Happy New Year written on top. But I am just not up to it, so, thankfully, Jacqui has agreed to make them. She is really an angel. You know she still hasn't found 'the perfect church' and I doubt she will as they are often filled with people like you and me! She is such an encouragement to me. She will be a blessing in any church where they recognize her gifts and abilities.

Unfortunately, online shops can't get me supplies of tissues and honey on Boxing Day, so I popped back to Wendleworth's this morning to buy mandatory supplies for the sick and infirm in my family. Notice it was me (also suffering) who had to go out – all the boys were at death's door.

Wendleworth's was like the grave but I did meet POG (Geoff). He looked worse than me and that is saying something! He said that his beloved also had the flu and was bedridden. I felt so sorry for him. He had a VERY detailed list of instructions from her – I now realize it's not Margaret but this new one – Aggie – the one he's going to marry. As we were talking, she phoned to remind him what to get.

Lord release POG from the chains of domestic oppression! AGAIN!

Talking about all things domestic – I have decided to hire a cleaner. The socialist in me shouts 'no' but the realist knows I cannot cope with three stinky teenagers and all their friends constantly trailing through the house. I feel like I am juggling delicate plates and they represent my life – family, work and church. I feel I have no time for myself, and my time with God is also just snatched at the moment because whenever I have a spare moment it seems there's another chore to be done. Clean the bathroom, tidy the sitting room, vacuum, sort out the kitchen. I know that we can have rest even in busy lives so I am praying that God reconfigures the rhythm of my life. I would like it to have a slower beat next year.

The boys are on notice – they WILL be responsible for tidying their own rooms from now on, even if it means they can't open their door because they are drowning in their own junk.

In general I am content, just physically tired. Jack does try to help but he is so busy just now with a new project. Let's pray life will become more manageable soon.

I thought it was hard when the kids were small. I remember living through several years of fatigue with little people keeping us up all night. Jack and I looked forward to a time when the kids slept through and we could have nights of passion. Now we head up to bed saying how much we love our beds and just fall asleep!

So if you are feeling sorry for me, please pray an angel comes round with all manner of goodies to make me feel better. Chicken soup and grapes would also be appreciated. Some gossip magazines and chocolate even more so! I really cannot slim or swim when I feel like death warmed up.

Louise – sneeze, cough, splutter . . .

PS Am praying that the outbreak of family illness does not result in another flood of lasagnes. Nothing yet.

Date: 28 December

✉ Dear Lou

Sorry to hear the whole town is plagued with the lurgy. I just got an email from Sam and he, too, is suffering. Lots of xxx. ☺
  So sorry I can't come round. I can, however, send you Naomi's fabulous chicken soup recipe, a family heirloom recipe from Ken's mémé. It's meant to have special (healing?) properties to help you fight infection. Even I can make it! And I have chocs – boxes and boxes of chocs courtesy of generous gift-making clients – at home if you want to get someone to nip round to mine.
  On the domestic front, I think I might be able to help. Janette has decided to launch a new company and she's going into cleaning. Garry always wanted to keep her at home and she felt that was the only skill she had. So, rather than being depressed, she's turning it to her advantage and is now armed with cleaning equipment and rubber gloves. I'll bring you her leaflet when I get back (I helped her with some publicity and apparently she's already picking up some business). There are many people in your position – busy lives and not enough time to get all the basic stuff done without working themselves to death.

E

✉ Dear Esther

It really is that time of year when everyone is ill. Do you remember the Christmas when the kids were small and we had to take it in turns to stay up with them because all the adults in a mile radius were ill? The boys were the only people who didn't have the virus. That's because they had their daily spoonful of honey. You all laughed at me insisting on that little 'housewife's tale' remedy and I know I am not medically minded but I had read that it helps. And apparently, it did! Anyway that was an awful Christmas. Most of the turkey ended up in the bin.
  That's great about Janette. Maybe I can persuade Jack to agree

that we take her on. It would help her out and certainly help us. I feel the only place I can go for a clean, peaceful retreat is my en suite and (sometimes) my kitchen. And what's happened to Garry?'

Lou (Desperate for a cleaner.)

✉ Dear Esther

Stop giving Lou ideas! (Laptop left on so hacked Louise's email.)

Jack

📧 Dear Lou

Did Jack tell you he emailed me and told me off for giving you 'ideas'? Check your 'Sent' box on your email.
　Janette and Garry? Well, it's definitely all over. He had been sniffing around again but she is being strong. Given that he is now having to support not only her and their two kids, but also a set of twins in Brazil (Yes, Jose's sister gave birth to twins . . . a double whammy!) I don't blame her. I think she still cares for him but he ended the marriage and I think, at last, she's seen him for what he is.

E

✉ Dear Esther

I've been in touch with Janette and she's agreed to do some cleaning for us. She's delighted and I am delighted. A great New Year's present for us all! Thanks. Just sitting down with a cuppa and the obligatory Christmas showing of *The Sound of Music*. Safe journey. See you soon.

L xxx

21

SUBJECT: HOLY HANDS

DATE: 5 JANUARY

✉ Hi Esther

I think I am beginning to lose it . . . certainly wondering if I am OK on the HRT. Glad to say that the night sweats have eased a little, but I am still doing stupid things. The boys would say I have always done stupid things, but now I'm beginning to wonder if they are right. Maybe I need more medication?

This morning, I dropped by Wendleworth's to get a few supplies, including tights. I always forget them and never seem to have any when I need them. I haven't a clue where they are disappearing to – can't be the boys borrowing them!

Anyway, walking across the car park, I saw a young man try to nab a disabled bay that an old lady was trying to reverse into. I was mad, and went across to speak to him.

'Why did you take that lady's space and WHY are you are parking in a disabled bay?' I moaned. 'Don't give me an excuse about it being busy – you should NEVER park in a space that has been specifically allocated to those who are not capable of walking distances and need to be near the front of the shop. It's outrageous! Don't argue with me. You don't have a leg to stand on!' I screamed.

The young man opened his door and said, 'Lady, I can assure you I do actually only have one leg I can stand on.' I looked down to see that he had an artificial limb! If I hadn't been so angry I would have seen that he had one of those blue disabled badges prominently displayed on his vehicle.

There were lots of apologies and I crept round the shop in stealth mode hoping not to see him and thanking God the boys weren't with me as they would have creased themselves laughing at my expense. I was so keen to leave, I forgot half the things on my list.

Oh, and to top it all, as I ran, head down, to my car, I passed the old lady's car – she had found another disabled space – and she did NOT have a blue badge. Oh dear. I need to start praying more for the gift of patience!

However, my stress levels are down on the domestic front. Janette is great! I can't believe she agreed to come in on 2 January after our mad New Year. She is a GODSEND!

She has done wonders to the house already but objects to even stepping into . . . not the boys' rooms . . . but Jack's study! Yesterday he was working from home and she did something I've never really been able to do without it sounding like nagging. She told him off!

She later told me she felt sorry for me trying to clean a house, run a business and cope with all of Jack's 'rubbish'. Jack thinks she should be on her first verbal warning – secretly, I would swap that for praise.

She is a complicated character. On the one hand, she put up with Garry making unnecessary demands and refusing to allow her to go out to work for so many years. On the other, she's prepared to tell off MY husband. Maybe she's just got more courageous lately.

I do envy you just having to clean up after only yourself. Our house constantly needs cleaning up after all the visitors!

Louise

PS So how was New Year's Eve? We were so busy talking about Canada the other day I never did get the low-down on what happened. Not the details anyway.

🖃 Dear Lou

At least you get lots of visitors even if the majority of them are uninvited teens!

New Year's Eve? NOTHING happened. Well not really. What do you expect from a joint church social and watch night? Sorry you guys couldn't make it. I missed you! We had a pleasant evening and yes, Sam was there, along with quite a few from Hope & Light.

Sam was looking quite suave actually. I told you, didn't I, that he picked me up that evening with a lovely bunch of roses? It made a change from another box of chocolates. It felt like I was swimming in them when I got back from Canada. The blooms are really gorgeous. I've attached a photo so you can see they were not red but a lovely yellow.

I am going off topic – back to the social.

Garry was lurking in the corner and Janette (glad the cleaning job is working out by the way) and the kids were also there. Janette danced with Father Sean from St Peter's ... Garry was spitting teeth ... what was he thinking? Father Sean is at least 65 and he's a Catholic priest, for heaven's sake. Anyway, he was only being polite. He spent most of the evening at Rev T's side. They seem to be quite good mates, which is fantastic. It must be quite lonely being a single female vicar!

We had the candlelit watch-night service, which took us through midnight and into the New Year. During the service Rev Tracey got us all to hold hands. It wasn't quite a 'Bind Us Together' moment but it came close. Sam and I had gone into the church together so yes, we did hold holy hands. I could swear Rev T winked at me when she gave the instruction! On my other side there was POG and his new young woman, so I also got to hold hands with Geoff! Delightful!

Aggie, by the way, is an odd little creature. I'm sure you've seen her – she works in the community library. She wears her hair in a bun and looks about 50 although she is only about 35, as previously reported. She comes across as quite quiet and mousey but I think she's got Geoff wrapped around her little finger. Or under the thumb – take your choice. Apparently, when Angela passed away Geoff took to going into the library for company and their eyes (his framed by new specs) met over a shelving unit.

They're getting married in February.

Back to the watch night.

Rev T gave a little message and got us all to think about the year past and the twelve months to come. I know this year is going to be another upsetting one, what with Ken and Naomi and Mum back in Canada. Sam gave me a tissue! Not exactly the most romantic moment of my life. All snot and hankies.

And it was all rather complicated by the fact that halfway through Sam's moments of consolation, my phone 'beeped' and there was a text from Matt – Ken's brother – wishing me a 'Happy New Year' with a couple of kisses to boot.

Sam didn't see it. But everyone noticed that my phone beeped in church.

Esther

PS At the moment I'd swap having to clear up after a family any day. My little house may be neat and tidy but when the door closes it's awfully quiet!

PPS Have you discovered who the phantom tights stealer is yet?

✉ Dear E

So what's this with Matt? I guessed from what you said that you hung around together quite a lot over Christmas. But what's with the kisses? What are you not telling me?

Is it true that James turned up at the social and watch night with another woman and Catherine broke down in tears? That sounds awful – not just after the gossip, but you didn't say! It is just so sad and insensitive. As you know their eldest Bella has been spending more and more time here since she and Bobby started 'going out' but I didn't like to ask her. Talking of break-ups, did I ever tell you about Mum's bridesmaid?

On her 25th anniversary Alice and her husband arranged a party and a great meal for their nearest and dearest at a hotel. Mum said there must have been at least 100 people celebrating with them and they looked so happy. She said Alice looked stunning – new outfit, hair done, etc. They held hands and looked set for their journey to the Golden Wedding!

However, at the end of the evening when nearly everyone (apart from Mum and Dad) had left and they were packing the gifts into the boot of the car, Alice's hubbie suddenly announced that he'd had a lovely evening but was not going home with her. It took a while for it to sink in. Mum and Dad were standing nearby with their coats on ready to say goodbye and saw the look of shock on Alice's face.

Mum took Alice aside, while Dad quizzed her husband. Then, all of a sudden, Dad decked him! That's my dad – the quiet godly man!

It was completely out of character. Mum (and Alice) were astonished and Alice's husband (I can never remember his name) picked himself up from the ground and walked away. Alice came home to ours that night and Mum and Dad sat up all night with her. She was beside herself with shock and the next morning Mum had to take her to the GP. She stayed a week and then went to her sister's. Husband left the marital home within days and they eventually got divorced.

But – to tell your wife you are leaving on your silver wedding anniversary? That's just so harsh and a terrible thing to do. I know that relationships end for a whole range of reasons but there is a time and a place to make the break, surely, and you have to be careful not to hurt people. There is really no need, is there, to be mean for meanness sake?

A mad Louise

🖃 Dear Louise

I can't remember you ever telling me about it. SO sad!

Now about Matthew – well, we DID get on VERY well over Christmas. He is a hunk, and it's always flattering when a 'handsome dude' as my mum calls him, trying to be 'hip', pays you any attention.

Yes, he WAS around a lot – helping Ken and Naomi to move into their new home. Yes, we did spend a lot of time together, including that snowboarding afternoon and the ice skating day. And Christmas.

I told you, didn't I – he ended up driving me to the airport? For some peculiar reason neither my little sister nor my dear brother-in-law were available. And Mum is not driving over there yet – too much snow for her.

And yes, Matthew DID give me a peck on the cheek and a bit of a hug when we parted, and said 'hope to see you soon'. And yes, he has emailed a couple of times since I returned. And yes, we have spoken on the phone – twice.

But, as you pointed out to me when we met the other day, Matt's in Canada. Sam is here. Both are great guys.

Sorry not to update you on the James/Catherine situation. Trying not to be a gossip, but since you asked . . .

No, it was the other way around. Catherine was accompanied to the social and watch night by a very, very nice-looking gentleman whose name, I think, is Ian. He's a solicitor.

James arrived with the kids because he had them over New Year and he looked like a little lost soul. He spent most of the evening trying not to notice Catherine and her new man and avoiding half a dozen voracious single women. Sam rescued him quite a few times and then also came under their attack. Just outside the ladies' loo one of them – a woman called McKenzie (is that a real female name?) who is one of the beautiful people from St Michael's – asked me if I was 'with Sam' or if he was 'free'.

What was I to say? I didn't want to lie but was I going to leave Sam to her clutches? I said nothing but smiled quietly and sort of shrugged. Was I right? Was I wrong? I think Sam saw/heard what happened because he came out of the gents just as I was shrugging.

Esther

✉ Dear Esther

Sounds like a bun fight! I can always provide more buns. There are always one or two rejects from the ovens at Arkland Street . . .

Now I understand something Sam said to me at church yesterday. I asked if he had a good New Year's Eve. He said it was 'lovely' and that you had been 'amazing' and had 'rescued him' but he needed to speak to you about it. I wondered what he meant by that. Now I know. Thanks. He doesn't give a lot away, does he? That is a man thing I think. I am generalizing a little, because Jack is quite open about his feelings – well at least he is now – but it's like pulling teeth getting the full story from the boys at times.

So, despite the Matthew 'situation' – is there any follow-up?

L

🖥 Hi

Yes, yes, yes! Sam has asked me out. We're going to have dinner the day after tomorrow! Not sure if I'm excited or not. Not sure I can cope! What happens if he wants to become more 'serious'? What would I do about Matthew? Even though there's nothing with Matthew! Why can't I make up my mind? What shall I wear? Ahhh!

E

PS Feeling a bit like a spotty teenager again.

✉ Dear Esther

Calm down dear! Although I am over the moon it is only dinner, you're not signing a pre-nuptial. It may just be what you need – a friendship with possibilities.

I am happy to be your Gok-Wan consultant for the day. Does this mean a shopping trip? There is a great new shop in town that sells end-of-line clothes. Jacqui told me that's where she found her lovely purple jumper. Very reasonable, apparently.

Must go and tell Jack about the date – he will be thrilled. He told me just the other day that Sam was a 'man's man' and would make someone a great husband.

Which reminds me, he also confided in me that when he went into the flower shop to get me my Christmas bouquet he was accosted by Jason who, he noted, was wearing a lovely Christmas jumper that matched the plants around him – he was sorting out the poinsettia display. He says Jason was all over him like a rash, complimenting him on his slimmer physique and saying he thought he looked 'fit'. Jack said he mumbled something like, 'Marathon, hard work, got to keep fit for the FAMILY AND WIFE!' and fled in fear.

As you know, Jack has been avoiding the flower shop since the summer but at Christmas there was no option. Like a true OO7 he had cased the joint and had lurked around outside trying to establish whether Jason was inside. But for those wretched poinsettias he would have seen him.

By the way, Jason passed his love onto us all but secretly, I think he had just one member of the family in mind.

Lou

DATE: 7 JANUARY

✉ Hi again

Not sure I need any new clothes but just some advice. Casual jeans and white shirt? Or smarter? Bearing in mind it may be freezing so the ski jacket may have to be aired again.

E

✉ Esther!

OH NO, not the neon multi-coloured ski jacket! That smart red coat is very trendy and you look great in it. And take that new handbag – the one you got with your nice new luggage bought with your 'I Love Jesus' bag compensation money.

I am happy to give fashion advice as I am so up to date with the latest fashions! ☺ At church the other day I had some nice comments about my grey coat – the one everyone at home said made me look like Paddington Bear. Admittedly it IS a sort of duffle coat but it was a great charity shop bargain and looks nice when it is accessorized.

So jeans with a smart blouse and maybe a plain cardigan. And the red coat. Understated but smart is great.

Lou x

DATE: 8 JANUARY

🖅 Hi Lou

You know, I still wonder where my little 'I Love Jesus' bag is and whether it's being loved by the evil person who stole it. I fear it ended up in a dumpster but I just don't want to go there in my mind.

So I got home from work yesterday to find a call from Tom on my answerphone. I told you he emailed me while I was in Canada, and I did put him straight – that I was only on holiday and not emigrating permanently – but that, as I'd indicated before, I felt it was all over for us.

But there he was on the answerphone anyway. He didn't want to start the year without checking I was 'OK'. After everything that happened at the tapas bar and the airport, he still can't give it up.

What in the words 'I don't want to be with you any more' does he not understand? Should I meet him again, or email, or just ring him to say, 'Please leave me alone ONCE AND FOR ALL'?

E

✉ Dear Esther

He must still care for you – after all you were together several years!
But if you want my advice, I would not meet up with him. Do not
give him hope when there is none.

   I am coming to the conclusion that I don't know what goes on
in the minds of men. It would certainly help me with my brood if
I did! One minute I think I understand them and then something
happens and I get it so wrong. The boys are the worst. I have
found myself empathizing with them over broken relationships
and trying to offer motherly love. And then the next minute they
tell me it's not the girl's fault, they have to change – and ask
her out again! Are we breeding a whole new generation of very
demanding and manipulative girls/women or has life always been
like that?

   Jack and I have decided to sit the boys down for another chat. This
time it's on serial dating. We think that if they go from one girl to
another, committing to a girl then breaking up and moving quickly on
to another . . . and another . . . and another . . . then those habits could
travel with them into marriage. I hope they all believe, as we do, that
marriage is for life. Ollie told me the other day that he was praying
about who he would marry in the future. And Bobby told me just this
morning that he and Belle are now officially courting'. Very grown
up! I thought language like that went out in the 1950s! It's good to
know they can be serious at times.

   But Jack and I think that if they get into the habit of easy
break-ups, it's not good for serious relationships. Not that we want
them to dive into a long-term relationship TOO early, just that they
understand that any relationship should be worked at.

   You know this is not a dig at you. I know you have seriously
thought about Sam and you were very committed to Tom. I think you
have handled your relationships with integrity. Just saying . . .

   With love

A serious-sounding Louise

🖻 Dear Lou

I rang Tom. I agonized over what to do but decided in the end it was best to speak to him rather than email or meet him in person.

He's moving back to town . . . that's really what he rang to tell me, I think, when he left the message. It makes sense I suppose, to move back nearer his mum and work, but I honestly think he's blocked out the tapas and airport moments and still believes he'll be able to pick up where we left off.

So, once again, I told him just to accept that we would never get back together. It is OVER! I've MOVED ON! He did get angry when I said that and he mentioned Sam and asked if HE was the reason that I was acting this way.

I was so angry – he's had girlfriends since we split, even if they didn't work out. Did he think I was just going to sit around and wait until he had 'sowed his wild oats' and saw sense and then take him back?

But I stopped myself from being sharp with him. What I said was: 'I'm not in a relationship with Sam, he's just a very good friend. But that's beside the point – whatever my situation, please understand MY FUTURE DOES NOT INCLUDE YOU!' Not sure he has accepted it but we'll see.

I didn't bother to tell him about Matthew the hunky Canadian. That would have just been cruel.

I'm so tired of all this. It feels like we're back at high school and it's all 'I fancy her/does she fancy me?' I realize now that the age difference between Tom and I probably did matter. Have decided I really don't want to be permanently attached to a juvenile.

But I've been praying about it and trying to discern God's will in it all. Also asking for his peace at my decision.

E

DATE: 9 JANUARY

📧 Dear Louise

I was coming back from a meeting yesterday and I was on a train and there was this couple. They were having such an argument. They were doing it quietly and trying to be discreet, but I was sitting opposite them and so heard it all. She was wittering on about a maddening habit he had – not sure what it was, I didn't hear that bit. He was pretty much ignoring her while giving me the eye, and also smiling at another girl sitting a bit further down the carriage. I averted my gaze, but I'm sure his other half noticed his flirting.

And it suddenly hit me. Given that just a few weeks before he left Tom had been swearing undying love for me, then he departed saying he no longer loved me, then this 'love' suddenly reignited when he thought I was emigrating and I wouldn't be around to starch his shirts, I'm absolutely convinced that it wouldn't have lasted.

Twelve months ago exactly, I was looking forward to the YEAR WHEN I WOULD MARRY THE MAN OF MY DREAMS AND LIVE HAPPILY EVER AFTER. Imagine if we'd got married and he'd discovered a few months in that he was no longer in love with me? I could now be facing the YEAR WHEN I WOULD GET DIVORCED!

I've not heard from Tom since our last phone conversation.

Esther

22

SUBJECT: TOUGH CHOICES

DATE: 10 JANUARY

✉ Dear Esther

You sound so positive just now. Well done for dealing with Tom once and for all.

I could do with some of that. I had to give Jack an ultimatum. ALL day I waited for some sign of recognition. I can sort of understand when he missed the fact that I had lost a stone in weight. I can be kept wondering for a day or so when he misses the fact that I have new glasses. But the sin of all sins – to go from brunette to blonde and not even a peep.

It all started when I called in to the hairdressers yesterday for a trim. I told them I wanted a makeover and they told me about this new hair colouring system that just happened to be on special offer. I know the cost of these kinds of treatments goes some way to cover the national debt, but cupcakes are in and we are in profit after Christmas and New Year . . . and they had a cancellation, so I sat down in that chair. You would have been so proud of me. Spontaneity! Change of hair colour and at least three inches cut off the tresses. Tomorrow I am collecting my contact lenses.

But from Jack, no mention of the change, even when I tossed my head from side to side at dinner . . . Mary the dog gets more attention than me. ☹

L x

PS Sending a photo.

✉ Beautiful L

WOW! How brave. The Twitpic looks fabulous! You're gorgeous anyway but now – IS JACK COMPLETELY BLIND?

Tell him if he doesn't behave, and if he and the boys don't start coming out with some compliments soon, then I'll come over and assault them with my ski jacket.

E

DATE: 11 JANUARY

✉ Dear Esther

Thank you for your kind comments. I told them what you said. It worked! I am now a happy bunny. All male members of No. 22 Arkland Street are in the good books today. I've had lots of positive feedback and even had a bunch of flowers from hubby. He ventured forth and bought them from the flower shop, even risking being chatted up by the attentive Jason!

We are off out for dinner tonight. A little bribery can be nice when you are at the other end of it. Jack told me I look better than my new range of cupcakes.

Better a cupcake than a whole Victoria sponge.

L x

DATE: 12 JANUARY

✉ Dear Esther

Guess what? In the post today I got a really nice card from Darcy. When I opened it a voucher fell out for Avina – that new spa near Clethorpes House.

She sounds much happier and tells me she has got involved in her local Baptist church.

God really does answer prayer!

L x

🖃 Dear Lou

Well done Jack! Well done Darcy!

Good news all round. I had a call from Sam. Another dinner date next Saturday. All these meals out are not good for the hips. I've been thinking I need to join a gym, perhaps one with a swimming pool. However, I fear that although I'll start with good intentions at the end of the day it'll only be the pool that gets any use. I heard something on the radio the other day – this guy was saying that he reckons about 95 per cent of those people who get all 'I must get fit' at New Year and then sign up at a gym will not be regularly working-out come February.

E x

✉ Dear Esther

Rather than a gym membership, why don't we check out the local swimming pool and get a year's subscription? The leisure centre does a deal on swim only or a small range of classes. Don't need to sign up to everything. I was by there the other day to pick up Bobby from his badminton and I saw they have something called 'Aquasize', which sounds intriguing. What do you think?

I also have a new recipe that I want you to taste. It is for tiramisu cupcakes. You can have just one cupcake for breakfast and you have your morning caffeine shot! Actually I think they do taste lovely and I don't even like coffee. Another recipe for that book I may write. Jack likes these new inventions, so that's a good sign. Just not sure what to frost them with or if a sprinkling of coffee powder is enough!

So pleased to hear you are officially 'dating' again. Do you want my voucher? You need to sparkle for Sam. ☺

L x

🖃 Dear Lou

Thanks. Not sure about the sparkling. My nose is still a bit red from the Canada wind and snow. But what's make-up for, after all?

Talking of Canada, the news from there is great. Mum is fixed on a flat in the retirement complex – it's called Haven Village.

It's still snowing.

Mum's flat is on the market so if you know anyone needing a new home ... Didn't you tell me that Janette might want to downsize?

Also heard again from Matt ...

Aquasize sounds fabulous. Let's check it out.

E

DATE: 13 JANUARY

✉ Hi Esther

I forgot to tell you that Janette and Garry are back together. I saw them in church last Sunday. The girls are OK. They are young and can probably cope with all the change in their lives. Difficult, isn't it? I think we can be so selfish in the decisions we make. Did you know that Garry originally left the night before Molly's birthday? She woke up on the day of her birthday and her daddy had left. How bad is that?

Good news though, Janette is at least carrying on with the cleaning business. I have to say I was relieved to hear that, because when I saw them together my first (selfish) thought was, 'Oh no! I hope I don't lose my cleaner!'

She explained when she came in to clean on Tuesday. I have to say I was speechless.

How crazy is she? What's that all about? Where is her self-respect? I understand she wants to save her marriage, but he went and left her for six months – it wasn't just a day playing golf! He disappeared and produced two additional children! What does that teach their girls? However, he has managed to worm his way back into Janette's affections.

It's beyond my understanding.

Janette did let slip that she worries about Garry – apparently he's so handsome that other women can't keep their hands off him – and if she takes him back he'll be 'safer'. Have I missed something? I can't see his appeal myself. Also, I think character makes the man, not necessarily a good profile, and after the way he's behaved he's very unattractive in my eyes.

But Janette obviously cares for him and is willing to take him back. She tells me he's repentant and has come back to the Lord. She's forgiven him, and he appreciates how tough that must have been for her.

It reminds us of someone else who loves us, even though we wander off to do our own thing. He's always waiting for us to ask for forgiveness and journey with him.

So maybe not so radical after all?

Lou

☐ Dear Louise

I think that's very brave of her. Maybe Janette can't face the future alone. I pray it works out for them. As you say, we have to keep believing that there is hope even for the hopeless.

E

23

SUBJECT: EMBARRASSING MOMENTS ALL ROUND

DATE: 17 JANUARY

✉ Dear Esther

I know it was me who suggested Aquasize but I did not relish the thought of stripping down in public and really hoped you would be there to give me some moral support. However, as the weight loss has slowed down and African children stand to suffer, I gave it a go. You ARE a chicken not coming along. I know you had an excuse but . . . really . . . why on earth you thought a reception at the House of Lords stood above an hour of ferocious splashing around in the council pool is beyond me. By the way, hope it went well!

So it was an interesting evening but one that I will not, unfortunately, be wanting to repeat, at least not unless I have dyed my hair (again), lost loads more weight and had plastic surgery.

The people were friendly, the instructor motivated, the water warm and everyone was dressed up to the nines. Don't laugh, it's true – they all have very nice swimming gear.

This was just like a posh gym – everyone competing for the 'best-looking exerciser' title. I could see right through them – and every one could see right through me!

My costume was transparent.

Yes I didn't buy a new one – trying to save money and all that. It's a shame, because if I had done so I could have saved a LOT of egg on the face. My humiliation surpassed even the Fairtrade egg incident.

I got changed and I had even remembered my swim hat . . . thankfully it fitted, although I had forgotten how hard they are to put on. I struggled for about fifteen minutes trying to ram my brains and my hair into the rubber monstrosity. Why on earth do they make them like that?

Then I headed to the pool and got involved in the class.

It was sheer hard work! Lots of pushing against the water with arms, legs and bits of my body I'd forgotten existed. Everyone else seemed to know what they were doing – I think I was the only 'new girl' even though it was the first class of 'term'.

The instructor was a bit like a boot-camp bully. She repeatedly yelled stuff like, 'Come on ladies . . . you can do better than THAT!' 'Push, push, push! Spread those legs!' 'Deep breaths . . . and . . . push!' It's a long time since I was in a maternity delivery room but suddenly I was back there and, as on those occasions, I just wanted to yell, 'Give me some drugs! Gas and air! Anything! Just make this pain go away!'

Class over, legs like jelly, I staggered back to the changing rooms. Everyone else was happily chatting but I hadn't got the energy and I'm afraid I was so quiet no one even asked me my name.

Thank goodness!

As I ambled behind them en route to the lockers ready to have a quick sit down on the seat before I could summon up the energy for a shower, I passed that huge mirror near the toilets. Why on earth they put a massive reflective object there I'll never know – just where you can see yourself at the most unflattering of times, exhausted from the energy you've expended in the pool, or legs crossed rushing for the loo.

Anyway, as I passed it I caught a glimpse of myself in the mirror. Hmm . . . well . . . to say my costume was transparent was an understatement. I may as well have not been wearing any clothing at all. And I'd been like that for a good hour. I'd wondered why I'd had some weird looks, especially from the (male) lifeguards who at one point were at the other end of the pool. I just thought it was because I was a particularly poor Aquasizer and I was prepared to shrug off that humiliation. When I realized that the world could see bits of me that even Jack hasn't caught sight of for a while, I was mortified.

I wrapped myself up in a huge towel. One kind woman tried to comfort me, explaining that swimsuits can 'thin with constant use'. I did not want to tell her that the costume was bought for my honeymoon nearly twenty years ago and has probably only had a couple of dozen 'airings' in that time.

I do not think I have ever got changed so quickly. I am now very grateful for that ridiculous rubber swim cap because hopefully no one will recognize me when I go out without it. I covered my head with the hoodie from my gym outfit. Yes I have a gym outfit, which Jack bought me when I started to lose weight. It has been worn exactly five times, including this trip to the pool.

I didn't even shower, but wrapped up and dashed home to the solace and privacy of my own en suite where I enjoyed a very long bubble bath. Followed by a glass of wine and a large slice of Jack's birthday cake.

So next week, when Aquasize is on and those lovely ladies are parading their beauty and expertise, I shall be thinking of other ways to lose the pounds.

Lou x

✉ Dear E

I know it's the middle of the night but I've been awake for hours thinking about the transparent costume and I now realize that I've been parading around in it all year. There was last year's Valentine's break – can't remember whether I swam or not. Then there was France – I did dip into the pool there so WHY did Jack not tell me my outfit was ridiculous? Or did he not notice?

Louise

DATE: 18 JANUARY

🖃 Dear Louise

Picked up your messages. So sorry to hear about the embarrassing pool incident. I know it's easy for me to say, but try not to think about it . . . it's all water under the bridge now . . . Everything seems worse in the middle of the night! Hope you got some sleep.

Seriously, sounds hideous and all in the name of getting fit. Not fun!

If the Aquasize class is that competitive I may have to reconsider my future exercise regime. And I'll certainly check out the condition of my 'cozzie' if I do decide to go.

This all puts me in mind of a girl at secondary school. She came from a rather puritan background I think, because she was very self-conscious about her body. Most of us were quite happy to expose a bit of flesh from time to time. Whenever possible, once beyond the school gates, it was skirts folded up from the waistband, so they ended just below our intimate bits and school shirts released from the captivity of our knickers and tied in a knot under our busts to expose a little midriff. Very glamorous!

This classmate, however, was very different. I don't think I ever even saw her knees. She put on thick tights to wear with her sports gear. The only time when she could not cover up was during the weekly swimming class, which must have been sheer hell for her. What with that, and all the girls wandering naked or half-naked around the changing rooms. It must have been torture.

Although it was an all-girls' school she remained embarrassed. I never did find out why, and I can't remember her name now. Isn't that terrible? All I can remember is her nickname – 'Plaster Girl'.

One day someone let slip that they had seen her changing for the pool and did we know that she always covered her nipples with plasters before putting on her swimming costume? I remember thinking that was hilarious at the time but then feeling rather sorry for her. We weren't a family of nudists or anything, but I wasn't ashamed of my breasts, not even at that age – when I didn't really understand anything about my body.

Mind you, over the years when I've caught a glimpse of myself in a mirror wearing a tight sweater on a cold day I've understood the significance of the plasters – if you know what I mean.

Must go – I'm about to have a Skype call with Naomi and the boys.

Isn't technology wonderful?

Esther xx

📧 Dear Louise – again

Just come off Skype with my little sis. She just wanted to tell me about a new job she's been chasing. She always said that, given an opportunity, she'd go back to nursing and she's pretty much managed to secure something part-time that fits into her busy family schedule (she pronounced it 'sked-dual' – she's losing her English already)!

I think she has to do some refresher course first but hoping to go back to work in the spring, hopefully when all the snow is gone in a couple of months.

Kai and Kenny Jr were jumping all over the place and speaking half in French, half in English. I always thought it was excellent that Ken and Naomi insisted on that bilingual thing at home and it's paying off. However, I think I may have to go back to French school if I'm to keep up with those little monsters!

Why I'm writing though is – Naomi wanted your recipe for velvet cupcakes. Can you send it to her please? She won't take any business away from you, she promises, but she's having a houseful of people around from church next weekend and wants to impress them. Yes, you heard right – church! The family has started attending regularly again and have found a lovely group of new friends there. I'm SO thrilled! I'm going to fire off an email to Mum now.

E xxx

⊡ Dear Louise

Sorry – me again. For the second time I forgot to say – the House of Lords was magnificent. We had the reception in a lounge with a balcony/terrace overlooking the River Thames. It was a bit chilly out there by the water but most of us at the event braved it – just to be able to say we'd been out on a terrace at the Houses of Parliament!

The 'do' was organized by one of my old clients ... well not old ... former. I was thrilled to be invited but a little surprised, as we parted company some years ago and she went with a much larger London-based PR agency. She's now working on some big campaigns to promote women in business.

Anyway, during the reception she took me aside and the upshot is she is very interested in me working with her again. The fancy PR agency didn't quite work out for her – they didn't understand her or the way she operates.

We're due to have a meeting in the near future. Very exciting.

Esther

✉ Dear E

Wow, that is wonderful! Well done!

When you're very rich and famous will you still have time and space for a small client specializing in cupcakes?

Do any of your clients need cake for their functions – very good at delivering batch orders with green frosting!

L ☺

 Always time and space for you Lou! See you soon!

24

SUBJECT: FINE DINING

DATE: 21 JANUARY

✉ Dear L

Are you there? Want the details? Hellloooo?

E

✉ Dear Esther

Of what? What have you been up to?

(innocent) Louise

✉ Lou

Ha Ha.

So it went well. Second meal out in a fortnight. We went to that friendly Italian in town. It was a lovely evening. It did feel strange though. The last time I was in there it was with the ex . . .

The staff welcomed me like a long-lost relative. One of the waiters even winked at me as he poured my sparkling water! I ducked behind the menu and mumbled something about the starters. Sam was quite amused. I really don't remember much about the food but the conversation was great.

Sam is such an interesting and kind man. Did you know he has been a couple of times to Uganda to help a rural community with water and sewerage projects? What a great thing to do in your holidays. That and Christian bus tours. Do you remember, he went by coach to Spain last year and the group stayed in a monastery for a week? Sam told me this was his first 'Grand Tour' and, I suspect, his last. He reckoned it was 'different' – it wasn't necessarily designed as a singles only holiday but, although there were a few couples, the majority were unattached, and it turned into something of a week-long speed date that was, in his case, highly unsuccessful. None of the single females were under the age of 65! But the monastery, he reported, was very relaxing and the scenery spectacular.

We talked about loads over dinner. We always find so much to chat about. I do think we were last to leave. He dropped me home and yes . . . we had a little smooch. ☺

You'll get more details on Friday over coffee and cupcakes – you ARE bringing the cupcakes, aren't you? I feel I could now attack a red velvet without the memories of my break-up and a sobbing ex-future-mother-in-law giving me the shakes.

And yes – I am fine . . . it was fine!!

Esther xxx

✉ Esther

Save your kisses for Sam! Sounds like a great evening.

So is Matthew off the scene?

I sent Naomi the red velvet recipe and she reported back that they went down a treat at her house group.

As you know I'm constantly tweaking recipes and I've swapped the cider vinegar to lemon juice in the red velvet cakes. You know they are becoming more popular, and they are certainly my favourite . . .

Just thought you would like to know.

Lou

⌑ Dear Louise

Sounds scrumptious. I don't really care what's in those cakes . . . just ensure they taste yummy.

Yes, Naomi was very happy all round. She even managed to persuade brother-in-law Matt to make an appearance and he didn't collapse from the strain of being surrounded by a bunch of Christians.

I know you're going to think I'm terrible but I'm still in touch with Matthew.

I'm still not sure whether I want to jump into another serious relationship with anyone at the moment . . . I'm actually enjoying just being paid attention to by two lovely men.

And yes, I DO heed your warning – Sam is a lovely man and a Christian. Matthew is also great but NOT a Christian . . .

Yes, I do get the sense of what you said the other night. Do I want to get into another relationship with another non-Christian?

Maybe that's my problem, always going for the ones who aren't quite right. Not exactly 'bad boys' but certainly not ideal partner material? I know I've sworn off non-Christian men but tell my hormones and my feelings that!

Funnily enough, although Mum would love me to get together with a Christian, and she really likes Sam, whenever we speak or she writes, she's constantly asking if I've been in touch with Matthew. I think she really just wants me over in Canada!

Anyway, that's not why I'm writing. Got to tell you something that happened at work on Friday.

You know how I've moaned about the women on my team constantly disappearing to have babies, which leaves me with a costly recruitment nightmare.

Well, the married who's been with me for a while and was due to have her fourth baby has, unfortunately, suffered a miscarriage.

Obviously she had to have time off, and I felt terrible because I secretly felt like she was letting me down by producing another sprog and inconveniencing me. But, bless her, she took very little time off and was soon back.

On her return she asked to see me and she was in tears. Not particularly about the baby, although that was obviously upsetting. But because, as she said, she was so grateful that she had such a great boss.

She actually thanked me for being kind to her, for understanding all her commitments with the other three children, for not getting mad when she announced baby number four, and for being so understanding when she suffered the miscarriage.

I didn't know where to put myself. I felt such a fraud. After moaning endlessly to you about her and the others and my 'poor business' I wanted to scream, 'Actually I'm a terrible person, please don't thank me!' I didn't do so, of course, but just said something like, 'Well I'm here for you!' and offered her another tissue. I'm praying God will forgive my hypocrisy.

But that wasn't the end of it. The praise kept coming: 'I've never worked for a Christian before, and I'm so glad I'm working for you.'

If only she knew … but it's good to know that despite MY weaknesses, God has used me as a witness, albeit unwittingly!

Esther

DATE: 22 JANUARY

✉ Dear Esther

I will say no more about the Sam/Matt situation. At least not until next time it comes up! LOL

Guess what? Something unbelievable happened today. I was clothes shopping – more new tights. I've discovered who's been ruining my supply. It's that Mary dog – she's moved from socks to tights and she is going to be the death of me and my budget.

Well there I was looking at the range available when I was approached by a total stranger and asked if I wanted to do some modelling!

At first, I wondered if it was because of the new air of confidence I have, being a new me. I'm back on track with the weight loss. Then I wondered if this proposal was a little, you know, dodgy.

Well it's not. Apparently, there is a new women's wear catalogue coming out and they want models for it. It is for women of a 'certain age and size' and I was a bit shocked to be approached because I'm aware that I am not the world's best looker.

But needs must. Despite the recent run on red velvet cupcakes, I've scrutinized the business accounts and we do need more orders if we are to keep afloat. So the extra cash for the modelling could come in very handy. I am going to give it a go.

I will let you know how I get on. Not telling Jack just yet. I don't want him worrying about the business – hence the email rather than a call. Don't want him knowing.

Will let you know when my first shoot is.

L x

✉ Dear Lou

Shoot YOU more like! This is SO exciting!!

Don't put yourself down. You're gorgeous, especially since that fabulous new hairdo. I told you, it took years off you. Not that you looked old . . . oh you know what I mean.

Putting my 'sensible' hat on, though. Do you not think you should tell Jack? He might be a bit surprised when you pop up in ads and billboards!

E

✉ Dear Esther

I don't think the catalogue will go global, but I understand what you're saying. I'm going to tell him tonight. Don't want him having a fit. The boys are out so it'll be a good time. Laurence is at football and then is having a sleepover at his friend David's house. Ollie has put Chloe behind him and has a new girlfriend, although he hasn't yet told us who she is. He's managed to keep her secret – not even Laurence and Bobby can find out. They think we are naïve sometimes, but as parents we always find out – we have our ways!

Bobby is out with Bella. Did I tell you that when she was round the other day she broke down in tears? She has taken the split between James and Catherine really badly and she really doesn't like Ian, her mum's new man. Actually, she hinted that he's virtually moved into the old marital home.

I haven't seen Catherine at church recently, although James is still a regular. He really looks like a lost soul. I felt so helpless when poor Bella started sobbing. I just hugged her, mopped up her tears and gave her cake. I suggested she speak to her mum and dad about this but I'm not sure she will. Poor little thing.

As always, a marital breakdown doesn't just affect the two people involved.

Louise

DATE: 27 JANUARY

✉ Good morning Esther

I'm in the bad books with Jack. He really doesn't want me to do the modelling.

I chose my moment – tucked up on the couch with his favourite beer and the football on TV. I thought he wouldn't really be paying attention and that, later, when the deed was done I could honestly say, 'Well I TOLD you about it! It is not MY fault you don't listen to me!'

But I got it wrong. He not only heard me, but he put down the beer and switched off the match.

He knows better than to say, 'You will not do it' but he made it clear that he didn't want me to go anywhere near a photographic studio.

I got really upset and said stuff like, 'Don't you think I'm pretty enough to be a model?' and, 'So you think I'm fat and ugly, do you?' which left him with nowhere to go.

He just said, 'Don't be ridiculous! I just don't want MY WIFE parading her body in public.'

What does he think . . . that I'm going to be a transparent swimming costume model? Oh no, I've already DONE THAT!

He became completely unreasonable and I ended up ranting: 'It's OK for you to go out in skimpy shorts and parade in front of the WHOLE WORLD but not alright for me to be celebrated as a beautiful woman!'

Jack snapped back, 'The only time I've been out in "skimpy shorts" recently was for the half-marathon . . . was it MY fault that the WHOLE WORLD was watching, as you say?'

Instead of seeing the funny side of this argument, I was on a roll . . . I then threw the sad lack of appropriate marathon attire back in his face . . .

'And look what it got you . . . a bout of ridiculous MAN FLU!'

Suffice to say, it all went downhill from there. The result was, I'm afraid, that on our only Friday night in months when the house was our own (the boys all staying with friends) and we could have had passionate moments in any room of our choice, Jack ended up sleeping in Ollie's room!

OK, so we would not have had sex in every room but that's beside the point. We broke that golden rule: 'Never go to bed on an argument.' And I feel awful. Jack's gone out running this morning and I'm waiting for the boys to return. And feeling sorry for myself.

L ☹

✉ Dear Lou

So sorry to hear this . . . but I'm trying to look at this logically. Did you actually TELL Jack what sort of modelling it was?

Esther

Dear Esther

I read your email and . . . well the penny dropped.

When Jack returned, and he'd had his shower, I greeted him with a mug of breakfast tea and a pile of toast. And an explanation.

YOU WERE RIGHT!

Although he's known me since junior school, when he heard 'modelling' for some reason he had this vision of me in my underwear in one of those lingerie catalogues. WHY? Does he not know me at all?

Anyway, when I explained that it was a women's wear catalogue and the nearest to skimpy I would get would be an outfit that would not include a cardigan, the relief on his face was obvious. I then told him I would also be able to keep all the clothes I model and his face positively glowed! Quids in!

And we made up. He's coming to the shoot. I am hoping he will not get in the way.

Thankfully, the sun has risen and peace reigns again in Arkland Street.

Thank you, God.

Louise xx

DATE: 29 JANUARY

 Dear Esther

The news from ours keeps getting better. I got an email this morning to say that Lou's Cupcakes has been nominated for Cupcake Creator of the Year. I'm guessing that it was someone in Christians in Cake who nominated me/us, but I don't care. It seems that, unbeknown to us, a few of the judges have already ordered and consumed some of our products – mystery cake buyers and eaters – and we are to be invited to a fabulous evening in London next month where the winner will be announced.

I can't believe this – one moment I'm up to my ears in debt and self-pity, the next I'm being asked to model and I'm up for a prestigious award. Even being nominated should make my business fly. Jacqui and I are already thinking we might need to take on new people. Meanwhile, Ollie has said that his new girlfriend might be able to help. He hasn't told us who she is yet, so that might be a problem!

I really need some help, though. The Creative Bakery Awards people are going to announce the nominations next week and it's going to be in the papers, etc. I need to know what to do if I'm asked for any interviews.

Lou xxx

 WOW Lou! Fabulous news! Coming round now. Don't worry, I'll be your 'PR'. . . I'll handle press for you and ensure you make the most of this great publicity!

25

SUBJECT: PENNY'S FROM HEAVEN

DATE: 31 JANUARY

Dear Lou

Did I mention that Penelope and Clive are coming down for a few days? They're due tomorrow and Penny rang to ask if they could stay at mine.

As I've said before, they're not short of a penny or two (no pun intended) so I've no idea why they want to lodge with me for two nights. Could they not get a hotel room? There's a cheap hotel that advertises with a duck that they could have booked.

Apart from the fact that I've got to whizz round and clean up, the other thing is ... they've not long been married and the question is – what happens if they get up to ... well you know ... The walls of my little house are quite thin. It's surprising, isn't it, that these modern houses aren't made like the ones of old? When Mum came to stay last year I could hear her blowing her nose in the middle of the night.

Anyway, I've no idea why I'm stressing about this, but the thought of lying awake for two nights listening to my guests making sweet love in MY big bed doesn't fill me with joy.

And what if they start making out in the lounge. I told you what happened when I visited them in the Lake District, didn't I? Every time I entered a room there they were, entwined!

I know that was soon after the wedding, but what happens if the passion is still upon them? Where will I put myself? My little living room is so small we'll be basically sitting on each other's laps, which could be very awkward if they're all over each other.

Esther

✉ Dear Esther

Don't panic.

How long is it since they got married? Eight Months? Nine Months? Chances are they've exhausted the first flush of love. But that's what comes of getting married so quickly after meeting – all the excitement coincides with the early days of marriage. Whereas after long engagements those early wedded bliss days are just spent recovering from the wedding day.

Seriously, don't fret. I'm sure it will be OK. Doesn't Sam provide an insulating service? Might be worth asking?

Alternatively, they can stay at mine. Just say I offered and have a spare room.

Or . . . I still have those earplugs that I used on the flights to and from New York. You are welcome to use them, although they are second hand.

Lou x

🖹 Dear Lou

That would be fantastic. The offer of the accommodation for Penny and Clive that is, not the ear plugs!

It would save me worrying.

E x

✉ Dear Esther

I phoned Penny to give her my address. She actually confided
in me that she was not sure whether to book a hotel or not but
she thought you might think they were being rude. She is really
looking forward to seeing you and has warned us that they have
the wedding video!

Lou x

PS Thanks for the help with the Cupcake Creator of the Year
publicity. That article in the local rag was just fantastic. Jacqui and
I have been cooking through the night to fulfil seven new orders! At
this rate I might need to open a shop.

DATE: 2 FEBRUARY

🖥 Dear Lou

Thanks for dinner last night. What a great evening. Really enjoyable.
Clive and Penny are really good together, aren't they? Their running
commentary of the wedding was so funny. Even though I was actually
there I found it amusing!

As I explained after their big day, despite all our rude comments
about what sort of wedding Penny might have, it was quite normal really.

However, what I hadn't realized was that they really HAD
applied to be on that TV programme *Don't Tell the Bride*, just for fun!
I nearly wet myself laughing when Clive said he had actually planned
a Caribbean-themed wedding because he knows Penelope loves that
part of the world. I just kept thinking of *Pirates of the Caribbean*!

I'm so pleased for Pen though. It looks like third time lucky!

Thanks also for understanding about Sam and not insisting that
he was my 'plus one' for the night. I didn't really want to complicate
matters ... too many Penny questions. I haven't told her (or indeed
many people) that we're sort of seeing each other.

I wonder why that is?

Actually I've been thinking about Sam ... although I've known him for a year or thereabouts and we've had some lovely evenings out and some good laughs, and a little kiss or two, I don't really know much about him. He's never mentioned previous girlfriends or fiancées or 'significant others', although I can't imagine that he's got to 37 (yes, he is younger than me but ... not by much ... what's six years between friends) without having girls throw themselves at him. He's a successful businessman, good looking and a great guy. So why isn't he married?

The problem is, I don't really feel I can come straight out and ask him.

Imagine it – he arrives at mine for coffee and I sit him in the comfy chair and shine my reading light on him.

'Mr Jackson. Question One. Have you ever been married? Question Two. WHY haven't you ever been married? Question Three. WHAT are you hiding?'

See my dilemma? If I quiz him, it might make him run for the hills but it also might make him think that I'm interested in him ... which I am ... but not ... well maybe not ... that seriously ... yet.

Oh dear.

E x

✉ Dear Esther

Penelope could be Penelope Cruz! (Pirates?)

As for Sam – I've been wanting to ask you why you don't want to spread the news far and wide. You know, it is not a bad thing to let your emotions show a little, although I do understand that you don't want him to get his hopes up too high.

I have known Sam for a few years since he joined Hope & Light and I have never known him to have a girlfriend.

Lots of women, I think, would like to get to know him better. They do hang around him like bees around a honey pot. But, as you know, he is quite shy really and, while he is always friendly, I've not ever known him to have a twinkle in his eye for any of them – well not, at least, until you.

He is close to his mother, I believe, but he doesn't live with her and he doesn't strike me as a 'mummy's boy'. She is a member of St Peter's and he was brought up as a Catholic.

You know, we women are odd, aren't we? Society is odd, isn't it? Perhaps he hasn't yet met Miss or Ms Right . . . have you thought of that?

A 'woman of a certain age' is allowed to remain single while awaiting the arrival of 'The One' and the world barely bats an eyelid. But a 'man of a certain age' decides to avoid marriage and long-term commitment until the perfect woman turns up and we wonder about him. Is he – well, as the now departed blessed Angela might have put it in a lowered voice with a tilt of the head – 'the other way inclined'? What's wrong with him? WHY isn't he married?

It's such a long time since I had any man, apart from Jack, interested in, me so I cannot honestly give you any advice on when to approach Sam on this subject. But I do think you should get it cleared up.

We should chat about it sometime.

Are you still on for shopping? The boys and Jack are all out this Saturday – going to the big match. So once I've cleared up everything they leave in their wake when they have finished preparing for a day out at the footie – warm clothing, flasks of tea/coffee, packed lunches, etc. I'll be free.

I really need to get Darcy a present for her birthday. She is quite difficult to buy for. I was thinking of something bespoke. Need somewhere that sells unusual things. Any thoughts?

Let me know.

L xxx

DATE: 3 FEBRUARY

🖅 Dear Louise

You're right. I do need to get this sorted out. It's been really bothering me.

The reason this came up was because in a recent Skype call Matthew and I were chatting about the past. He reminded me that he was divorced, like he thought I should be clear about his 'situation'.

Of course, I knew that and I have known him longer than I've known Sam, although not well. We've only met each other sporadically, like at Naomi and Ken's wedding and when he visited them here in the UK a few years later, and holidays back home to Canada – and of course this last Christmas. But it made me realize that I know so little about Sam.

Shopping would be good. I need some new boots.

Not football boots!

E xx

PS Re Darcy's present – there are also some great online shops that sell really unusual bespoke presents that are not available in the main high street. Might be worth checking those out?

DATE: 5 FEBRUARY

✉ Dear Esther

Just need to have a rant. As you know, I spent two whole days last week making and decorating 150 cupcakes for Mr and Mrs Frederickson's silver wedding anniversary party – a last minute order, which meant I had to dip out on our shopping trip and spend my time up to my elbows in lovely sparkly icing. It was a real push to get the order completed because of the new business we're getting as a result of our Cupcake Creator of the Year nomination but we managed it.

I rang Mrs Frederickson to come and collect them and got no response. Eventually, three days after their collection date had passed and a bin full of cake (Jack and the boys could eat no more) Mrs Frederickson called round this morning. She explained that they had separated.

I had to make her tea as she struggled to share her news. After many tears, cake (a couple of our 'Mini Madeira Specials', which are proving very popular at the moment) she left. I didn't have the heart to ask about the bill for the cupcakes.

Although we are not doing badly, we are not out of the woods yet. I know Mrs Frederickson is heartbroken and I do feel mean thinking about it, but I can't afford to lose that sort of income. It is yet another consequence of relationship break-up. It reaches out and affects more than you realize.

Anyway I offered to pray for her and explained I go to church. I explained that I could not help in any other way but I know someone who can! Once I mentioned that, we had another flood of tears.

But I still want to 'share' the bill with her. Is that terrible? I'm praying about it!

Louise

DATE: 6 FEBRUARY

✉ Dear Esther

Forget my last moan. A cheque for double the amount owed for the Fredrickson cupcakes arrived this morning. I found it on my doormat. She must have popped it through the letterbox overnight because it was hand delivered.

The Fredericksons apologized for all the inconvenience they had caused. And there was a note from Mrs F explaining that the prayer must have worked – I presume that means they are back together.

Praise the Lord!

Lou x

DATE: 7 FEBRUARY

Dear Lou

I received a lovely present from Penny and Clive thanking me for the time they spent with me. It was a voucher to have my 'colours' done. Never had that done so I thought I may go just as long as it's not too extreme. All part of the revamp! I'm following your lead.

Esther

Dear Esther

I am so glad they were generous – we received a framed photo of the happy couple. Kind of odd! I am feeling a little green with envy but maybe purple or turquoise will suit better.

Louise

DATE: 10 FEBRUARY

Dear Louise

Update on Sam.
   So I plucked up the courage and asked him THE DREADED QUESTION.
   No comfy chair and spotlight, but we met for lunch today and he sort of opened the subject by talking about something that happened to him when he was teenager. He had been on a pilgrimage to Lourdes with his parents. As he was talking about his past, I saw this as my opportunity.
   Turns out he was an only child, and rather sheltered. His dad died when he was only fifteen and he really took over the 'man of the house' role. He didn't go to university (although I think he would have been quite capable of getting a degree – he really is

clever) but trained locally as a plumber. Although his mum certainly didn't expect him to stay at home and was always keen for him to find a girl, he only moved out five years ago, and he said he had never quite found that 'Miss Right', or at least one who would be interested in him.

I was astonished. Surely, I said, he must have had lots of girls chasing him. He laughed and said, 'Not exactly!'

Well, it appears that until about seven years ago Sam was rather overweight and even more shy than he is now. He worked very hard to lose the pounds and it took him four years to get fit and healthy.

When he had shaped up, every girl who had ever laughed at his inadequate attempts to ask them out and engage them in conversation suddenly not only wanted to date him, but were 'lining up', as his mum said. He dated a few, at least those who remained in the single club, but none floated his boat. He stopped going to Mass for a bit, because he felt uncomfortable being the only 'available male' in the parish.

Eventually – the result, as you know, of the joint churches' Men Aware meeting that Jack was leading at the time – Sam found his way to Hope & Light Church and, while Father Sean was disappointed that he had decided to move away from his Catholicism, he certainly wasn't going to excommunicate him. In fact, he encouraged him to get involved in another fellowship. That's ecumenism for you!

Sam is not a big talker and I think this was the most he'd ever said to me at one sitting. Lunch was followed by three cups of tea. With that unexpected blizzard we had overnight, we just stayed cosy in The Crooked Teapot, snuggled by the fire and chatted.

Oh, by the way, Janette is working there now, as well as the cleaning job. Apparently Garry still hasn't found any employment. You know he lost his job when he skipped to Brazil and he's just not been able to find anything 'suitable'. Janette reckons he's trying hard but 'people just don't seem to understand what he's worth'.

He earned very well in his previous job in insurance and he's determined that he won't take any employment that offers less. The job centre told him that unless he went for interviews he couldn't get his benefits. They sent him to various interviews, all of which were unsuitable. But the last straw, Janette reported, was the humiliation of being sent for a job as a shelf-stacker at Wendleworth's. He absolutely REFUSED to be interviewed by that 'boy manager'. He's lost his benefits, so Janette is working two jobs while Garry is now a 'house husband'.

I knew it would work out badly. Janette looks exhausted, but she's made her bed . . .

Anyway, back to Sam. I feel more at ease. And, I think, Sam didn't get any hint that I was asking him about his past with a view to being a part of his long-term future . . . well, at least I don't think he did.

Just about to head off to London. Back to Westminster. That old client is now a 'new' client and it's an enormous amount of work helping her promote her new Women in Business charity and she's hosting a big fundraiser tonight. Maybe you'd like to become part of it, now you are on the brink of cupcake world domination?

Glad I have Colin to hold the fort when I'm out of the office, and the account managers are both pulling their weight. Life is good.

See you tomorrow at the cake stall for Pounds for Africa. Still happy to help.

E xxx

✉ Hi Esther

I figured that Sam had been raised a Catholic (I think I remember him once telling me he sometimes goes to Friday Mass with his mum) but I wasn't aware of the details. As you say, he's not one to spill his guts to all and sundry. I can't imagine such a hunk was once a 'large' guy . . . just shows what we can do when we put our minds to something.

Anyway, glad you've got it all clear with the Boiler Man. Didn't I tell you there were no dark secrets?

L xx

◻ Dear Lou

Yes, yes, OK! Anyway, are you up for a radio interview about Cupcake Creator of the Year? Just heard from MixUp FM and they are dead keen to have you on tomorrow. I told you I was going to contact them. What do you say?

E

✉ Dear Esther

Only if you'll come with me. Never done an interview for any media people before. Bit scared! But . . . in for a penny as they say.

Lou

 Brilliant will sort out MixUp FM and let you know! Will hold your hand. E

26

SUBJECT: SNOWMEN AND REAL MEN

DATE: 12 FEBRUARY

✉ Dear Louise

Forgot to ask when we just spoke on the phone and now your line is busy. (Is that Ollie on the phone again?) Would you be able to take me to the airport?

I've managed to get tickets on one of those 'last chance' travel websites, although I've paid through the nose. Thank God for the new business contracts – this time last year business wasn't so great and a short notice trip across the Atlantic would have left me really tight.

So I'm flying out tomorrow and need to be at the airport at 4.30 p.m.

E x

✉ Dear Esther

Presumed Sam would take you but very happy to drive you.

No it was Laurence on the phone. He was talking to a GIRL! Never thought I'd see it.

L x

▣ Dear Lou

Actually prefer you to take me to the airport please. I feel so tearful and I know you'll cheer me up.

When I spoke to Naomi earlier she didn't really say much, only that Mum had fallen, broken her leg and was in hospital and was asking for me. Am I mad for panicking and just jumping on the first plane out?

Anyway, Sam is out of town. Remember he's gone on that church leadership preparation course?

E x

✉ Dear Esther

Sorry – of course . . . he's with Jack! How could I forget?

Of course you're not mad. You only have one mum! I know what I would be like if my mum or dad had a bad accident and I was miles away.

Have you managed to get in touch with Colin yet?

Shall I pick you up at 2 p.m.? Will give us plenty of time to get to the airport through this ice and snow. Then there should also be time for coffee before you have to go through passport control.

L

 2 p.m. will be great. Thanks! E xx

DATE: 13 FEBRUARY

▣ Dear Louise

Sitting in the departure lounge and there's free Wi-Fi. Hallelujah!

Thanks for dropping me off and for the fabulous box of mixed cupcakes. The family will love them, and Mum will absolutely adore the handmade get well card – you are clever! Sitting around has at least given me time to do some business online.

Emailed Sam to let him know what's happened. I didn't manage to speak to him yesterday – that conference centre must be out of mobile range.

You know I told you that I did get to speak to Colin, and he's going to hold the fort? Well, I forgot to ask you if you could hand over my keys when he comes round this evening? He will need to get some contracts that I've signed and are on my desk in my little office at home. Thank God for Colin.

My flight is being called. I'll text when I arrive.

Love to the family.

E xxxx

 Landed safely and on way to hospital.

DATE: 15 FEBRUARY

✉ Dear Esther

Hopefully you'll get this when you have had time to breathe.

We prayed for your mum and you and the whole family at our prayer group last night. I hope your mother's injury is not too serious . . . but you'll have a laugh at this.

We were in the middle of praying and I think our Rev had got the wrong end of the stick. I asked for prayer for healing for your mum's broken leg following an accident, the cause of which is still not known to you. I asked for prayers for you, as you were flying right at that moment to Canada to be with her – that God would give you peace. And Ditto for the rest of the family who are all very anxious, especially at this time when they are still settling in their new home.

Rev got a little mixed up. This is what he prayed:

'Dear God, we pray for Esther's broken head, which she had as a result of an accident while flying to Canada. God, please heal her and her family all of whom have no homes at this time. Holy Spirit, let peace and healing descend on this family, they are having such a hard time.'

I think he either needs a hearing aid, or he's changed the habit of a lifetime and has taken to the booze. Although we were meant to be very sombre and praying for you, some of us did start to giggle. I looked across at Jacqui and she had her fist stuck in her mouth trying not to laugh out loud.

I told you, didn't I, that after months of persevering with the church with the awful leaders, she has decided that a short journey to worship isn't so bad – it's Hope & Light for her after all! It's lovely for me to see her worshipping with us and everyone has been so welcoming. We try not to talk about work things in church. She's still dating her flour man, Brian, and has brought him along as well.

Oh, by the way, Suzie was also there at the prayer meeting. She is a nice girl. Still seeking but, I think, very, very warm to Jesus. She is at the point where she is wondering why he might be interested in her and has agreed to do an Alpha course. I won't have time to go and help or facilitate a group this year due to the extra workload, but have offered to make cake – an offer they rarely refuse. It's a way I feel I can serve.

Lou x

⌨ Dear L

Thanks to everyone for the prayers. Much appreciated. But here's something weird. Your Rev must be tuned in correctly or something.

You know when you're getting ready to disembark from an aircraft the steward/ess always says, 'And please be careful when retrieving your bags from the overhead locker because some of them may have moved during the flight'?

Well, those in the bin above my seat HAD moved.

Last-minute travel booking means I was cramped for nearly seven hours between Bald Man who snored very loudly and Busybody (large) Woman who wanted to talk throughout the flight, even though all I wanted to do was to watch the movie while trying to prevent Bald Man from drooling on my left shoulder. It was that new movie I wanted to see about slavery. I am just going to have to buy the DVD!

As soon as our plane had taxied to a halt and I had scraped drool off my jacket and shaken Bald Man awake, Busybody Woman asked me to grab her bags. I crawled across her large lap and opened the overhead locker. Her very large holdall, which in London I'd helped her cram into the luggage bin, fell out and hit me on the head.

So, when we got to the hospital (Naomi had arranged for Matt to pick me up at Quebec City Airport and take me straight to the hospital to see Mum) Matt first had to rush me in to the ER to have my head wound attended to. It's not much but I have a massive headache. Quite a lot of blood for such a small cut but they glued it together with ... well ... glue! So didn't need stitches. Amazing really. What will they think of next?

When I finally got to her, I found Mum to be 'comfortable'. She has a compound fracture and has her leg hoisted in a sort of sling. As she said, 'very ladylike'. She's also suffering from cracked ribs, but the collapsed lung is not causing too much of a problem.

Again, thanks for prayers.

Will report more later.

E xx

DATE: 16 FEBRUARY

✉ Dear Esther

What a relief! Glad your mum is not critical. But I think you made the right decision to go to be with her. As you say, it could have been much worse.

Hope the head is feeling better. It is great you didn't need stitches – they are so painful. It could have been so much worse.

I guess you're spending most of your time going back and forth to the hospital? But hope you manage to get some downtime and enjoy the stay as much as you can.

Glad the family liked the cupcakes – my pleasure. I told you they would travel safely. I'm becoming a dab hand at sending our products all over the place. Amazed you got them into the country! Thank goodness they weren't in your hand baggage, as it sounds like they would not have survived the cramped conditions of the overhead luggage bins!

Just had a thought. What am I going to do for the Valentine's Churches Together Quiz Night tomorrow? I was hoping you would be in my team. Jack is hopeless. He wouldn't know the difference between Amy Grant and Amy Winehouse, although he is hot on the sports questions.

I'm still cross with Jack for being away on Valentine's Day. Last year he took me on that lovely mini-break. This year he was on a church leadership preparation course. Did no one on the organizing group notice the clash? He left me a card and some flowers but Ollie was so caught up with his own romantic life that he forgot to give them to me in the morning and texted me halfway through the morning with the words 'Card and flowers in the garage'. Very romantic! All the boys got big cards from their beloveds – even Laurence, although he insists she's 'JUST a friend'! We still haven't discovered who Ollie's new love is.

Have I told you about the church musical that Hope & Light is attempting to stage? I am definitely not going to join in the singing – my voice would set the neighbourhood dogs howling. Anyway, it's based on the life of Job – so a cheery topic. We had a planning meeting last night.

One of the church members did a creative writing course last year so she was nominated to write the script. She told us that she woke up last week with the words 'does a good job' in her mind and feels that God has told her to base the musical on Job. I did want to ask if she has actually read the book and is aware of its less than upbeat content. Not exactly a subject to have the audience leaving with lifted hearts.

I volunteered to help with refreshments.

Are you still up to your neck in snow?

Lou x

📧 Hi Lou

That's hilarious. Isn't it funny what God tells us to do? He has such a sense of humour. I look forward to the production.

Mum is fine. It's the first time ever she's been 'plastered', being teetotal! She's getting loads of attention, including several of the retired gentlemen from the Haven retirement village who've visited her in hospital and brought her flowers. She hasn't even moved in yet but had been to a couple of the 'socials' in the past few weeks as she prepared to relocate from Naomi and Ken's granny annexe.

My mum – a romantic figure? Who'd have thought it? Her hospital room is like a florist's shop. Jason would love it!

Sorry to hear your Valentine's was awful. I have to admit I was also secretly a bit miffed when Sam told me that course would mean he would be away for the day, but he promised he would take me out when he got back. As it happened, it was the last thing on my mind this week. He tried to contact me on Skype on the day but it didn't work, what with my travelling and the hospital and his course, and the time difference . . . but he emailed to say there's a big card on my doormat and he is looking forward to treating me on my return.

E xx

✉ Dear Esther

Glad your mum is OK and didn't need an op! Let me know when you are returning. I'm guessing Sam will pick you up?

Attached is the shopping list for duty free as requested! Please could you remember to look for Cerruti 1881. Love that perfume. Or Beautiful. That's if you have space in your case. It sounds like you did a lot of shopping. Did you get Jack's message about maple syrup? His favourite breakfast at the moment is American pancakes and maple syrup. I have told him we can buy it here, but he is convinced that it is better coming from the country of origin.

I have also told him he will need to think of running a few more half-marathons if he is going to be eating pancakes and maple syrup every day. I was nearly hit with a frying pan. ☺

L x

DATE: 17 FEBRUARY

📧 Dear Lou

I was hoping to be back within the week but I think I need to stay a little longer. I want to stay to see Mum discharged from hospital and it'll be a few days yet.

Yes, Sam will be at the airport. What did we do without the internet? It's been a lifesaver for me while I've been here. Not only has Sam been in touch but business seems to have carried on regardless of me not being physically present in the office. I know I've banged on about this before but Colin is a bit of a marvel and I take back everything I've ever said about my account managers. They have all really stepped up to the plate and held the fort magnificently.

At first, we thought Mum might need to be in hospital for weeks, but she has bounced back remarkably and is already up on crutches. Kenny Jr and Kai think she's Wonder Woman! As you know, she was due to move into her new flat in the Haven Village about now but Naomi has persuaded her to return to the granny annexe for a little while longer. It makes sense – Naomi can keep an eye on her and nurse her back to full health.

The only thing is, she stands to be smothered with love. Ken's family can't do enough to help her and her own sisters – my aunties Tante Marta and Tante Lily have also driven over a few times with their families – my uncles and cousins and various wives/children/friends. I do think it was the right decision for her to come back to Canada. She has really been scooped up into the bosom of her family, as they say.

When she met my dad on that holiday in the Alps so many years ago, and moved from Quebec to the UK and made a life there, I guess she never thought that so many years later her youngest daughter would go on holiday to stay with the tantes in Canada, meet HER future husband (a college roommate of one of the cousins) and that their union would, eventually, bring them all back to the North American continent. As my beloved dad said at Naomi's wedding, 'You couldn't make it up if you tried!' It was MEANT TO BE!

Anyway, let me know how the quiz goes. Sorry I'm not there.

Esther

PS Love to everyone.

DATE: 18 FEBRUARY

✉ Dear Esther

Sam dropped by the other night. He's really missing you. Did he tell you I managed to strong-arm him into joining Jack, Jacqui, Suzie and me on my team for the Churches Together (late) Valentine's Quiz last night?

We could have done with you and your storehouse of random useless knowledge (your words, not mine!). You, I'm sure, would have known where Sir Cliff Richard was born, what Madonna's first top ten hit single was and the last movie that Henry Fonda appeared in.

However, at least we did not come last. There were 12 teams and we came in 10th. Mind you, one team had to leave early because they were all feeling ill (the Hawkins family – since discovered they are all down with winter vomiting sickness) and the team that came in 11th were all under 14.

Laurence was on that team. They got a prize even though they effectively were bottom of the pile. A reward for being the youngest competitors.

Oh and I've discovered who Laurence has been calling. It's James and Catherine's second daughter, Bella's younger sister Caroline. Thank goodness I've run out of sons because their third daughter Cassie is coming up on the inside rail!

Louise

📧 Hi Louise

1. Lucknow, India (Cliff)
2. 'Holiday' (Madonna)
3. *On Golden Pond* (Henry Fonda appeared with daughter Jane)

Haven't lost it. Still the Queen of Trivia.

Esther

✉ Dear E

HA HA HA HA HA HA

Yes, I know all that NOW . . . Just didn't know it on the day.

Lou xxx

📧 Dear Louise

It's busy here and, believe it or not, despite the distance, work is manic. I've even picked up a few business leads here in Canada.

You know in a mad moment or two I've wondered if I could work from Quebec, and maybe fly in occasionally and drop in to the

England office. There appears to be lots of work here for the likes
of me – small PR into charities, etc. A few of my campaigns, like the
Women in Business charity, are going to go global, I just know it.

Ken has been amazing. I think he realizes how much Naomi and
Mum and the boys miss me and he's been frantically trying to fix me
up not only with brother Matt but also with potential clients. The fact
that I don't have the right to work in Canada at the moment doesn't
seem to deter anyone. They think that would be a simple process,
given the fact that my whole family is now in Quebec. I'm not so sure.

Mum is back in the granny annexe but her stuff has arrived
from the UK and for the past few days I've been helping to move
everything into the new flat in the Haven Village. The break is healing
really well and she's hobbling around with help and crutches, but for
a day or two sat majestically like a princess in the middle of her new
'salon' in a big easy chair and commanded the moving-in operation.

She had already ordered some extra furniture from local stores and,
with all the bits she had containered from England, we have found a place
for everything in the apartment, which is now looking spectacular. Ken
and Matt were amazing, getting everything off the truck, lugging it through
the snow and hauling it up to the second floor. They had some help from
brothers Stephen and Paul, and my cousins Richard and Jean-Luc came
over and helped. My tantes were also there with food and directions.
They are funny. Identical twins, they've never lived more than a couple of
blocks away from each other, married brothers and have both had three
boys. There are a lot of boys in our family.

There is a lift in the Haven Village but some of the larger pieces of
furniture needed dragging up the stairs so we required lots of help.
But I have to say, on day one we did have a few too many people in
that little flat.

Mum's new apartment is simply beautiful. It has a huge picture
window that overlooks the lake at the back of the Haven. Even though
she won't move in for another couple of weeks – Naomi is determined
that she will be able to shower without assistance before she will let her
out of her sight – Mum has started to get involved in the events in the
Village and of course has already got stuck in at the local church. It's a

lively place and she's thrilled that Ken and Naomi and the boys have also got involved. It's been really good for Naomi, having a great group of new friends who she met at a music group which she's already enrolled little Kai in. What with that and all her sisters-in-law, she's barely missing her old circle back in the UK.

Mum loves being a 'proper Canadian' again, after forty-five years. She's slipped back into the lingo and is feeling really settled, despite the cast and crutches.

I remember when Naomi came back from that summer holiday in Canada and told Mum, Dad and myself that she'd met 'someone special' – a friend of Jean-Luc's who was 'great'. Mum was very excited at the prospect of having another native in the family. Since Dad died she's secretly yearned to be 'home'. She's happy. I'm happy she's happy.

As for Naomi, Ken and the boys, all is well. Ken loves his new job in the university marketing department – it really is a great promotion. Naomi is studying hard for her Back Into Nursing diploma and hopes to start work in the Spring. She's still on course to get into that nursing agency she spoke to before Christmas – they apparently have lots of what we would call 'locum' work on the books. In addition, Mum's accident might turn out to be a blessing in disguise for Naomi because during the hospital stay N managed to get to know and get friendly with quite a few of the staff. There might be an opening there as well.

Kai and Kenny are settling in well. Again, I say thank GOODNESS that Ken insisted on a bi-lingual home. The boys are already fluent French Canadian! You should hear them chatting away to their friends and cousins.

Got your list. I'll FaceTime you, shall I, for a chat? Rearranging my flight tonight.

Looking forward to seeing you all again. Although it'll be a wrench to leave the family – again.

Love

Esther

Fry not to worry about Mum. L x

 Oops – predictive text . . . meant try! L x

DATE: 21 FEBRUARY

✉ Dear Lou

I'm glad I came to see that Mum is OK but it has really emphasized just how far away my whole family now is.

She's been quizzing me about all the men in my life. She now thinks Tom is self-centred and manipulative. She was disgusted at the news of the airport punch-up last December.

Been spending a little time with Matt – mostly he's been helping to fix things around Mum's new flat. Although it's lovely, there were a few jobs that were needed doing. The kitchen cupboards had to be re-hung and he's also made some new fitted wardrobes in the spare bedroom. He's a brilliant craftsman. I told you, didn't I, that he's a master carpenter?

Yes, I have been in touch with Sam. Yes, he is missing me. But I remain in limbo land.

Some big decisions to make, I think! Prayer and fasting time.

How are Jack and the boys?

Esther xx

✉ Dear Esther

We're all fine. Half-term beckons so the boys are excited about our four days in Disneyland Paris next week. I am all packed already and ready to go . . . so busy I needed to get ahead of myself. I think it was ten years ago when we last went. It is an amazing place. I also remember that my feet ached last time so I am going with walking shoes. It won't bother Jack, he's so fit. I will get there one day . . . weight first then fitness level!

Jacqui is looking after the business when we are away in Paris. Orders are flying in and I think I said we are considering taking on more staff. I am thinking of making Jacqui my deputy manager. We may even need some business premises. Doing all the cooking in my kitchen is no longer appropriate.

And there is some even more exciting news. Since being nominated for Cupcake Creator of the Year, I have been approached about producing a cupcake cookbook. You know that I'm constantly coming up with new recipes and I had an email the other day from a local publisher. He heard me on MixUp FM and saw the article in the local paper, and then the MD remembered that he had been at a party where the main centrepiece featured Lou's Cupcakes. It might have been that big order at Christmas, for the hospital. Not sure.

Anyway, the upshot is that he wants one of their editors to have a meeting with me to talk about a recipe book. She asked me for some ideas, so Jacqui and I sat down to discuss what could be in a book and I sent through a draft proposal.

Along with new recipes I am going to have to think of names for some of the common cupcakes. At the moment, apart from some of the most popular – including your favourite red velvet – all our cakes are listed as numbers with a description. Sometimes when I listen to the phone orders I think it's like working in a Chinese takeaway!

Can't wait for you to get back so we can put our heads together. With your creativity and PR focus, I'm sure you'll have loads of suggestions for catchy cupcake names?

I thought the strawberry ones could be called Sam's Special or Strawberry Delight. How about those purple, orange and green cakes that Bobby loves so much? Maybe we could call them Coat of Many Colours cupcakes. And I'd really love to call my red velvet something like Esther's Delight.

Oh . . . and I saw Sam in town today. He looked a little glum. He is definitely missing you! He was wearing the new sweater you gave him for Christmas.

Jacqui and Suzie – who as you know shared space on Lou's Valentine's quiz team – swept him up last Sunday and took him out for lunch to cheer him up. Don't want to alarm you, but Suzie (I think) may be sweet on Sam and he certainly didn't turn down the offer of Sunday lunch at the Old Frog.

Louise

DATE: 23 FEBRUARY

📄 Hi Lou

I like Coat of Many Colours for the multi-coloured cakes – the colour of the icing reminds me of my bright ski jacket! But best not have one named after Sam right now. He's been in touch a few times. (About five texts and a phone call.) I remain confused.

How about Strawberry Scrumptious for that cake?

Matt took me out the other night to an ice hockey match and bought me a hot dog and a huge bucket of chicken wings, which, according to Naomi, was a highly romantic gesture – at least for the boys in their family.

Did I ever tell you how Ken proposed to my little sis? No red roses or kneeling down for him. They went to the Lakes for a long weekend and while canoeing on Lake Windemere he shouted back to her in the rear of the boat, 'Hey Sweetie, how about paddling through the rest of our lives together?' Romantic, those Canadian brothers.

Must go – my phone is ringing!

Esther

✉ Esther

Love this instant messaging . . . don't do this to me . . . what's happening? Your love life has more drama than ITV!

Hurry up and let me know what is happening. Your life is so much more exciting than mine!

Lou x

🗐 Hi Lou

Sorry about that. It was Colin, my new deputy director of business. That's his new title, I've decided.

He has some news. He's getting married and wanted me to know that the civil ceremony will be at Easter.

Now I knew Colin was gay ... I met his 'significant other' way back, a lovely boy whose name I can't recall right now. But ... married? Obviously not in church ... but I accepted the invitation. How could I say no? I have to say I've never given much thought to this subject, although I know it can be a huge minefield for some Christians. Need to pray over this. I want to support Colin, but ... why does life and faith have to be so complicated? More Bible delving is in order. Any help gratefully received.

But I am in a quandary and not just about that.

You know what they say, 'You wait for hours for a bus and then three come along at once'? No man action, then two fab guys come along. Matthew, Sam, Matthew, Sam ... What to do? I don't know what God wants me to do! I feel like I am in my washing machine whirling around and around.

A year on and more from the end of my only significant relationship to date, and after nearly twelve months of my wittering on about being content as a 'single', I think I should just sit back and enjoy being so. After the years with Tom I'm just beginning to get used to being on my own again, regardless of all the frustrations, the poor reactions of those around me and the confusing world in which I live.

One thing I do know – I am definitely happy in my own skin. Maybe that is simply what God wants from me.

Maybe the blessed Angela was right after all. Perhaps God doesn't intend me to be with either Sam or Matt – or indeed any man?

By the way – have you heard how Geoff and Aggie's wedding went? Can't believe they got married on Valentine's Day. How many months is it since Angela went off to meet the angels – five months? Haven't heard much about the wedding, but I have emailed Aggie at the library to explain that I had to fly at short notice to Canada because of my mother's accident, and I would not make it to their big day. To be honest it was the last thing I thought of when I heard about Mum's fall on the icy path outside church and I'd forgotten to contact Geoff and Aggie to explain why I might not put in an appearance. Not heard back yet. Maybe they didn't miss me.

Back to Sam and Matt. Yes, I have done that corny old thing – drawing up the 'for and against' list, which I know is a little ridiculous. But you know how I love my lists.

So I'm returning to the UK still rather confused. I'll bring some of that wonderful maple syrup back so Jack can have his American pancakes and we can enjoy a good old natter. I'll bring my 'Man List' and see what you think. Food and chatter with a friend – that's always a good combination and it's what I need.

Anyway enough about me . . .

Sorry I'm not there tonight to support you at the Creative Bakery Awards evening. Hope you and Jack have a wonderful time. You'll look amazing in that fantastic new little black number. Well done for losing the TWO STONE! You'll look simply wonderful when you pick up the Cupcake Creator of the Year award – I KNOW you're going to win!

With all that publicity AND a cookbook, the next twelve months promise to be exceptional for you and there's no one who deserves it more. How exciting! I want lots of photos from the evening posted on Facebook please!

The prize sounds great – a cruise for two. You and Jack deserve a great holiday. So prayers for your success!

Speaking of the book, thought of some alternative names for your cakes. Those red velvet ones could be called Heart to Heart or perhaps even Lou's Luscious Lovelies. Haven't got a thought yet about the marvellous Madeiran minis – oh, maybe that's it!

I need to get my thinking cap on. I'll get my team to it when I return. Colin is brilliant at catchy headlines and the like. Can you send me your list – the one that reads like a Chinese takeaway menu? I'm absolutely convinced that between us we can come up with some new and catchy cupcake titles.

Have you thought about what your cookbook might be called yet? Although these first ideas are a little cheesy, how about *Lou's Luxury Creations*? Or *Creative Cupcakes*? I know, they stink. Colin, I'm sure, will come up with much better.

Hope you are all well. Love to everyone. In addition to your shopping list, is there anything else you want from duty free? I will pick up Jack some aftershave this time – he was so miffed last time about not getting anything. What does he like?

Esther

PS Almost forgot to say . . . there's another wedding in the offing. I received an email from Rev Tracey last night. She's leaving Rivers of Life at Easter. Any idea why? She's getting married! Yes, you heard it.

Guess who she's getting hitched to? It's Father Sean from St Peter's! Can you believe it? This is a wedding I definitely want to go to. Obviously he's left the priesthood (kept that quiet) and with their age (she's just turned 69 . . . he's a few years younger) why wait?

She's asked me if I would be a bridesmaid! Actually I don't think it'll involve a flouncing dress, because the wedding will be quite small and quiet. I think it's more that I'll be her 'witness'. They want you to make the wedding cake.

It seems that God really does have a great sense of humour and that love does, after all, reign!

Love

Esther xx

A FEW EXTRAS

Coat of Many Colours Cupcakes

Multi-coloured cupcakes inspired by Esther's ski jacket.

Ingredients
110 g/4 oz butter or margarine, softened at room temperature
110 g/4 oz caster sugar
2 large free-range eggs, lightly beaten
1 tsp vanilla extract
110 g/4 oz self-raising flour
1–2 tbsp full-fat milk

For the frosting (the best bit)
140 g/5 oz softened butter
280 g/10 oz icing sugar
2 tbsp milk
Colouring to match Esther's ski jacket: bright green, purple and orange!

Making the cakes
1. Preheat the oven to 180 °C/350 °F/Gas Mark 4.
2. Line muffin tins with paper cases.
3. Cream the butter and sugar together in a bowl until pale.
4. Slowly add the beaten eggs and the vanilla extract.
5. Fold in the flour, adding a little milk until the mixture is of a dropping consistency.
6. Spoon the mixture into the paper cases.
7. Bake in the oven for 10–15 minutes until the cakes are a light golden-brown.

8. Remove from the oven and allow to cool for 10 minutes, then remove from the tins and cool on a wire rack.

Making the frosting
1. Beat the butter in a large bowl until soft.
2. Add the icing sugar and a little milk and beat until smooth.
3. Add the food colouring and smear liberally on the cakes. You might want to have each cake coloured differently, or the really adventurous among you might want to make each cake multi-coloured.

To serve
To avoid the glare please consider serving these cakes with dark glasses or ski goggles!

Lou's Luscious Lovelies

Those red velvet favourites!

Ingredients
250 g/9 oz plain flour
2 tbsp cocoa powder
2 tsp baking powder
½ tsp bicarbonate of soda
100 g/3½ oz butter
200 g/7 oz caster sugar
1 heaped tbsp red paste food colouring (alternatively, use beetroot!)
2 tsp vanilla extract
2 large free-range eggs
175 ml/6 fl oz full-fat milk
1tsp lemon juice

For the buttery cream cheese frosting
500 g/1 lb 2 oz icing sugar
125 g/4½ oz cream cheese (any type)
125 g/4½ oz butter
1 tsp lemon juice

Making the cakes
1. Preheat the oven to 170 °C/325 °F/Gas Mark 3.
2. Line the muffin tins with paper cases.
3. Combine the flour, cocoa, baking powder and bicarbonate of soda in a bowl.
4. In another bowl, cream the butter and sugar, beating thoroughly.
5. When the mixture is soft and pale add the food colouring and vanilla extract.
6. Gradually combine the eggs and dry ingredients into the pale mixture.
7. Finally, beat in the milk and lemon juice.
8. Divide this mixture between the 24 muffin cases.
9. Bake in the oven for about 20 minutes.
10. Remove from oven and leave to cool for 10 minutes, then remove from tins and leave the cakes to cool on a wire rack.

For the frosting
1. Put the icing sugar into a food processor and add the cream cheese and butter and mix until light and creamy.
2. Pour in the lemon juice and mix again.
3. Ice each cupcake.

To serve
Anytime, anywhere. Just because you can!

Just for Jack

Scrumptious and filling American pancakes.

Ingredients
135 g/4¾ oz plain flour
1 tsp baking powder
½ tsp salt
2 tbsp caster sugar
130 ml/4½ fl oz full-fat milk
1 large free-range egg
2 tbsp melted butter (cool slightly) or olive oil, plus extra for cooking

To make the pancakes
1. Sift the dry ingredients into a large bowl.
2. In a separate bowl whisk together the milk and egg, then add the melted butter.
3. Add the liquid into the bowl with the dry ingredients. Whisk until the batter is smooth. Let the mixture stand for a few minutes.
4. Melt a little butter/oil in a frying pan. When it's melted and sizzling hot add a ladle of batter mixture. Once the mixture starts bubbling, flip the pancake over. If you feel up to 'tossing' the pancake please feel free. But flipping with a spatula also works. Keep cooking and flipping until the pancake is a lovely golden-brown colour.
5. Use up all the batter until you have a nice pile of pancakes. You may wish to keep the cooked ones warm – you can do this by putting them on a plate in a warm oven. To soak up the excess oil/butter that may still be on the pancakes, place the pancakes on a piece of kitchen towel on the plate.

To serve
Serve with maple syrup – Canadian if possible. Yes, we know they are American pancakes . . . but 'North American pancakes' just didn't sound right!

Recipe for Life

On a more serious note, if you have just started going to church, been attending for a long time or never been but want to know a little more, this recipe is for you.

For Esther and Louise Christianity is so much more than attending church. It is not just a religion but a way of life. They allude to it when they discuss Easter.

Life Lines may be a novel and, hopefully, you'll have found it fun as well as thought provoking. But it's not just about church people and what they get up to, their failings and triumphs in life. Esther and Louise are entirely aware that left to their own devices they would probably fail to live 'a good Christian life'. They are both conscious that they need God in their lives and, although they may sometimes go off track, they want to know him more. For that relationship to happen they have come to understand the character and life of Jesus.

Truth remains. Jesus – God embodied in man – walked, talked and lived and then gave his life willingly for the punishment of our sin. Our previously fractured relationship with God the Father can be restored as a result.

If you are curious and want to learn more, please consider reading the first books of the New Testament in the Bible – the books of Matthew, Mark, Luke and John – and in those you will learn about Jesus.

We encourage you to come to understand the immense love God has for you and the extraordinary lengths he went to, to restore our relationship with him. Ask him to reveal himself to you and ask for forgiveness for that broken relationship. Take it from us – your whole life will change.

Notes

Exploring the meaning of life

The Alpha course is a course run by many Christian churches. It is primarily aimed at people who do not regularly attend church. There is often a meal, a talk and a discussion time where you can ask such questions as: What is the meaning of life? Why are we here? What is our purpose in life? Does God exist? Why is there suffering in the world?

Over the years Alpha and other courses that explain the basics of the Christian faith have proved extremely helpful to millions of people wanting to find out more about God and the meaning of life.

References

Beard, James, James Beard's American Cookery
(Boston: Little Brown, 1972).